Pictorial Guide to VASELINE GLASS

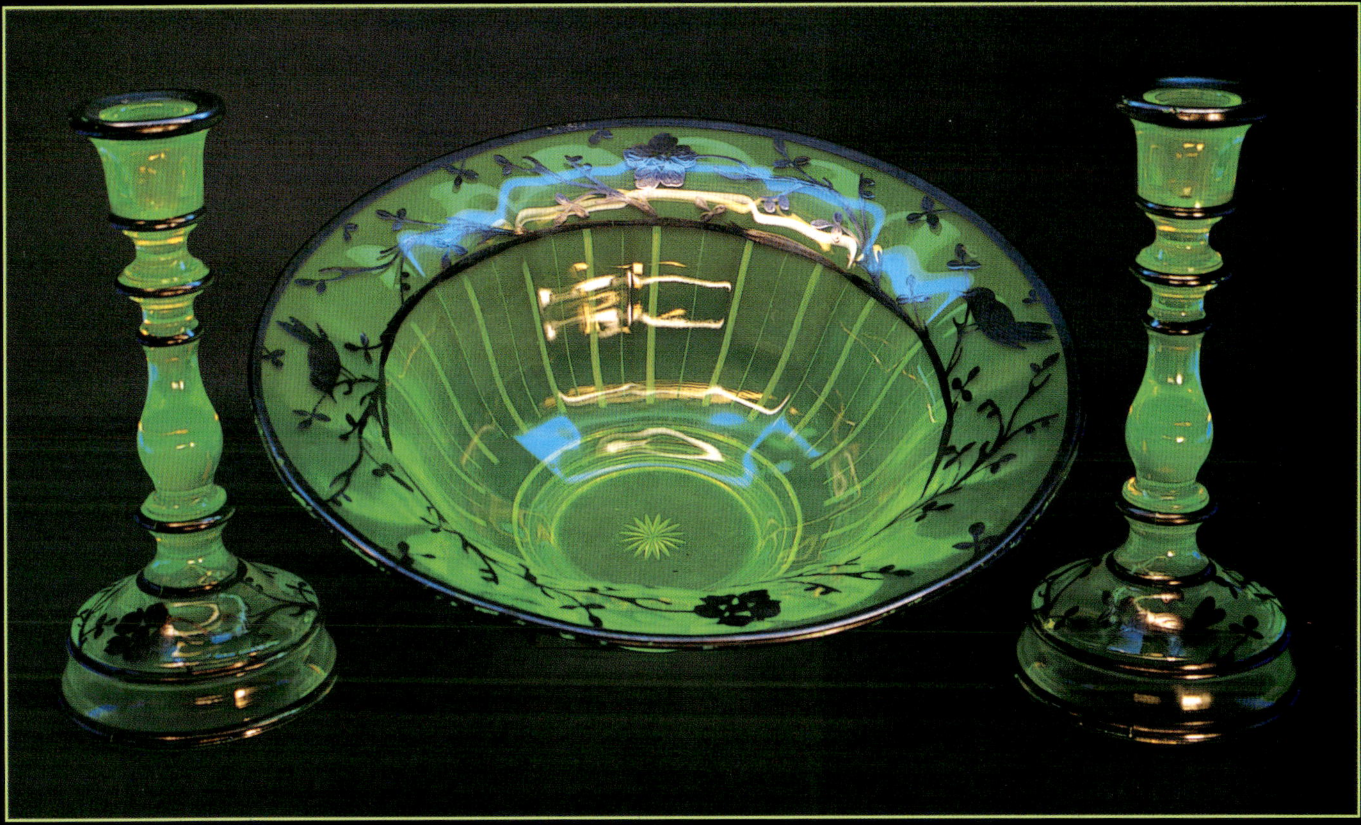

Sue C. Davis

Photography by Bill McFarling

4880 Lower Valley Road, Atglen, PA 19310 USA

Dedication

This book is dedicated with love to "the lights of my life," Amber Dawn Davis, my daughter; Ragan Dane Davis, my son; and Bailey Ann Davis, my granddaughter; and to the memory of my husband, Jackie B. Davis; my father and mother, Charles R. and Lucille Curtis; and my nephew, Chris Lee Davis.

Copyright © 2002 by Sue C. Davis
Library of Congress Control Number: 2002100293

All rights reserved. No part of this work may be reproduced or used in any form or by any means—graphic, electronic, or mechanical, including photocopying or information storage and retrieval systems—without written permission from the copyright holder.
"Schiffer," "Schiffer Publishing Ltd. & Design," and the "Design of pen and ink well" are registered trademarks of Schiffer Publishing Ltd.

Designed by John P. Cheek
Cover design by Bruce M. Waters
Type set in BernhardMod BT/Prose Antique/Souvenir Lt BT

ISBN: 0-7643-1644-3
Printed in Hong Kong
1 2 3 4

Published by Schiffer Publishing Ltd.
4880 Lower Valley Road
Atglen, PA 19310
Phone: (610) 593-1777; Fax: (610) 593-2002
E-mail: Schifferbk@aol.com
Please visit our web site catalog at
www.schifferbooks.com
We are always looking for people to write books on new and related subjects. If you have an idea for a book, please contact us at the above address.

This book may be purchased from the publisher.
Include $3.95 for shipping.
Please try your bookstore first.
You may write for a free catalog.

In Europe, Schiffer books are distributed by
Bushwood Books
6 Marksbury Avenue
Kew Gardens
Surrey TW9 4JF England
Phone: 44 (0) 20 8392 8585
Fax: 44 (0) 20 8392 9876
E-mail: Bushwd@aol.com
Free postage in the UK. Europe: air mail at cost.

Contents

Acknowledgments 4

I. An Introduction to Vaseline Glass 5

II. The Mid-1800s to the Early 1900s 11

III. The 1920s to the 1940s 53

IV. The 1950s to the Present 70

V. Vaseline Glass from Europe 93

VI. Uranium Glass 148

Glossary 157

Bibliography 158

Index 159

Acknowledgments

Sole credit for this book cannot be accepted by the author. It must be shared with family, friends, and publisher. Melanie Schonier, a true friend, deserves special thanks for the hours she spent assisting with research, pricing, previewing slides, and transporting glass for photographing. Also, thanks to the following for sharing their private collections, knowledge, and inventories: Catherine Conrady, Bruce Schiwitz, Cindy and Ben Burchfield, John Bell, Kelvin Russell, Red Roetteis, Glen Cheatham, Frank and Melissa Keathley, Ulrich Dollinger, Betty Kerr, and others who are credited throughout the book with their glass pieces.

My gratitude is extended to Schiffer Publishing for including my book among their high quality publications.

Once again, thanks to photographer, Bill McFarling, for a superb job. This book is as much yours as it is mine.

Last, but not least, thanks to my family who continually said, "You can do it!" when I despaired of ever completing this task and meeting my deadline—Amber, Ragan, Keri, Brendan, Rosa, Ken, Damon, Jana, Stefani, Molly, Connie, Ben, Snookie, and of course Bailey Ann who would have spurred Grandmama on had she been old enough.

Chapter I
An Introduction to Vaseline Glass

Welcome to my second book devoted to Vaseline Glass! When I began compiling my first volume, *The Picture Book of Vaseline Glass*, I wondered if I would have a sufficient number of photographs of different pieces of glass for an interesting book. I did! I then wondered if I could find enough different pieces of glass for a second book. Again, I did! The truth is that these two books only represent the tip of the iceberg as far as Vaseline Glass is concerned. However, together they are a good representation of the types of available Vaseline Glass. So, like my first book, this book is offered with two main objectives in mind, knowledge and pleasure. I am sure there are many of you, like me, who at times just enjoy relaxing and looking at pretty pictures of glass. I am equally sure there are times when you want and need information on glass. Therefore, this book, with its 508 photographs and as much information as I could find on each of the 600 different pieces of glass, is presented in hopes that it will provide the novice and seasoned glass collector alike with some knowledge and a lot of pleasure. As you are perusing this book, any additional help with identification would be appreciated since we all, as glass lovers, recognize that glass identification is an ongoing process of shared knowledge. Thanks and enjoy!

The Informed Glass Buyer

There is little doubt that many dealers of antiques and collectibles are thoroughly familiar with the items they sell. Still, in today's market, there are dealers who become involved solely because of the potential to make money in the buying and selling of old things. One can easily see this trend by observing the large number of flea markets, antiques malls, and collectibles malls where there are rows after rows of booths exhibiting various pieces ranging from recent to ancient vintage.

Collectors can observe the rise in antiques and collectibles shows that feature similar kinds of items. Sellers may or may not be interested in the specific names, patterns, ages, or location where the items they sell were made. This is not a critique of the current state of the antiques and collectibles market, but is a statement about the need for the collectors of glassware, whatever the time frame, to be aware of what they are purchasing. Often questions to dealers are answered with, "I'm not sure of what this is, how old it is, or who manufactured it." Even in some of the smaller antiques and collectibles auctions that take place, usually on a weekly or monthly basis, in communities around these United States, auctioneers will readily tell buyers that "they are purchasing items at their own risk." These auction houses usually make no claim about the authenticity of any object being offered for sale. The Latin term *caveat emptor*, "let the buyer beware," is very appropriate when purchasing antiques and collectibles.

As a result of this attitude in today's marketplace, collectors and dealers are left with the task of researching their own purchases. Books such as this one are very helpful in this process, since "a picture is worth a thousand words." I encourage collectors to observe and compare, as much as possible, the pieces of Vaseline Glass in their collection and those they find in their searches with the pieces in this book. One of my good friends in the antiques business always cautioned me when I said, "I have a piece just like that one!" He would ask, "Exactly like this one? Does yours have…?"

He was training me always to observe:
1. Pattern
2. Size
3. Color
4. Manufacturer's marks, labels, logos
5. Shape (especially the top edges)

Even though many shops and malls have signs that read, "If I break, I cry. If you break, you buy," one should always carefully examine glass for cracks, chips, "dings," or other flaws which make the piece less than mint condition. This examination process is particularly important when one is purchasing at an auction. Auction houses regularly remind buyers that they buy "as is, where is." This means the auction house will not assume responsibility for any flaws in the item purchased. Many buyers will get caught up in the buying frenzy even though they did not thoroughly examine the piece before the auction started. How many times have I seen sad faces when buyers have collected their purchases from the auction house and discovered a chip or crack? Too many to count! Glassware especially is in need of close examination because of the many possibilities for small cracks or chips that hide within the pattern.

Whether or not you are buying from a dealer in a mall, an auction house, a flea market, an estate, a garage sale, or an individual, please do not hesitate to take this book with you. Do not feel rushed to purchase Vaseline Glass because it "seems" right, or it "looks" good, or even because it is such a "bargain"! That "feeling" can quickly fade to disappointment unless you have done everything possible to protect yourself. You should always keep this book and a black light handy and use them when purchasing your next piece of Vaseline Glass. Pocket size black lights are adequate for testing fluorescence and can be purchased at lighting specialty stores, and on eBay. The pictures in this book are taken under black light. To assist the reader in recognizing this glass in the malls, antiques shops, and flea markets, a piece is shown below, taken under black light in the first photo and without black light in the second photo.

Once you have purchased that special piece of Vaseline Glass, a great deal of consideration should be given to displaying the piece in your home. Several of my collector friends have adopted my display ideas for their collections. Because of its versatility, I use my Vaseline Glass in all areas of my home. The beauty and elegance of this glass can be enhanced by the liberal use of mirrors. Its appearance can be subtly changed by the use of different lighting techniques. Exposed to direct sunlight, the glass will brighten a room with its brilliant glow. I like to keep a few small pieces in my kitchen window to brighten my day. Under fluorescent light, the glass is a sparkling yellow. A combination of fluorescent and black light produces a sparkling yellow with a hint of a fluorescing green glow. Black light alone gives the intense distinctive fluorescent green glow of Vaseline Glass.

I also use antique furniture to display my glass. With the addition of glass shelves, mirrors, and a combination of fluorescent and black lights, many different pieces of antique and modern furniture can be utilized as display cases. A few suggestions are china cabinets, pie safes, lawyer bookcases, wardrobes, old display cases used in dry goods stores, jewelry display cases, and glass enclosed stereo cabinets. Built-in, well-lighted shelves of

Dewey cruet with original stopper by Indiana Tumbler and Goblet Co., c. 1898. 5.65"h x 3.4"d. $165-195. *Courtesy of Kelvin Russell and Debra Jennings.*

glass backed by mirrors also are a good choice for display. Another unique idea is the use of a fish aquarium equipped with fluorescent and black lights. Displaying this glass is limited only by your imagination.

My quest for the beautiful, sometimes elusive, and often expensive Vaseline Glass has taken me from coast to coast. The value of my glass cannot be measured solely from a monetary aspect. Its true value comes from the joy it brings me. When I am tired, I can turn on the black lights, sit down, relax, and enjoy just looking at the glass. It never fails to make me smile when I flip the switch on the showcase. I hope you will find your own quest as exciting and rewarding as I have. Happy hunting!

About the Prices

The prices in this book are not intended to set prices, which are influenced by availability, condition, and economy, and which vary from one area of the country to another, from auction to auction, and from dealer to dealer. Prices in this book are for glass in excellent condition, even though a few pieces shown here have some imperfections.

A Brief History of Vaseline Glass

Vaseline Glass is the current name given to glass which has that yellow color of petroleum jelly. It is a transparent-based yellow to yellow-green glass. Over the years, many names have been used to describe this amazing glass. In the revised edition of Glickman's book entitled *Yellow-Green Vaseline!*, he states: "Before the 1930's there is no record of the name Vaseline having been applied to glass. This fact was confirmed in a conversation I had with Frank Fenton, chairman of the board of the Fenton Art Glass Co." The revision further states: "According to Mr. Fenton, Vaseline was being used by antique dealers in the mid-1930s, but no one knows whether a dealer or collector first coined the term." Other names for the glass include: Uranium Glass, Canary, Topaz, Yellow Glass, Lemon Glass, and Primrose. Norman Webber, in his book *Collecting Glass*, gave it the name "pearlene type fancy glass." In the book *Nineteenth Century Glassware*, Albert Christian Revi called it "lustered pea-spotted." Whatever the name, now it is glass that is highly collectible and enjoys increasing prices with each passing year.

Vaseline glassware, during the height of its production, served many functions ranging from practical to decorative. In the 1890s, Vaseline Glass was made in complete table settings and used daily. Other useful pieces were banquet pieces, lamps, doorknobs, medicinal bottles, vanity sets, decanters, drapery ties, and candlesticks. Some pieces, such as the novelties, were purely decorative. The popularity of these decorative styles reflects the growing interest by consumers, between the late 1890s and the 1940s, in decorative art glass. Much of the peak in art glass styles occurred between the 1920s and the 1940s, and coincident with each rise in consumer interest was the number of companies producing glass and the explosion of the pressed-glass industry around the world. Today the production of Vaseline Glass is limited to novelties and ornamental pieces.

How Vaseline Glass is Made

Vaseline Glass, like other glassware, as described on page 211 of the book *Glass* published by Intercon Arts, basically involves a "homogeneous mixture of inorganic compounds which upon cooling, form a random molecular structure rather than a crystalline one. It is in effect a super cooled liquid. The transparency of glass is due to the fact that there are no internal surfaces of a size approaching the wavelength of visible light. All glass contains silica from sand, soda, potash, and lime in varying proportions, depending upon the type of glass. There are four basic types of glass—flint glass, leaded glass or crystal, potash glass, and soda glass." Flint glass is colorless. It contains lead and potash. Lead glass is brilliant. It must contain at least 5 percent lead. Glass with 24 percent lead is considered to be crystal. Potash glass is hard glass. It contains potassium carbonate. Soda glass is generally light in weight and thin. It contains sodium carbonate.

The secret to getting the different colors in glass involves mixing the appropriate amount of each ingredient and firing the mixture at the correct temperature. Early on, glassmakers noted that by adding a small amount of uranium oxide to their formula, they could produce a brilliant yellow-colored glass. The distinguishing feature of this yellow glass is that it fluoresces a bright green when exposed to ultra-violet light (black light). All Vaseline Glass will fluoresce bright green when held to an ultra-violet light, but most yellow glass is not Vaseline Glass and will not glow. There are other types of glass that fluoresce a bright green when exposed to black light. Three of these, custard glass, Burmese glass, and Bristol glass are opaque glasses that fluoresce due to uranium sulfide in the formulas. Another is green Depression glass, a clear green-colored glass that was produced during the late 1920s and early 1930s by using uranium dioxide and iron oxide in the formula. Some dealers and collectors refer to the clear green glass of the Depression Era as Green Vaseline Glass since it will glow when exposed to black light. The author does not.

On page 34 of Neila and Tom Bredehoft's book *Hobbs, Brockunier & Co., Glass*, the following formula is given for canary glass (Vaseline Glass) with the units of measure being presumably in pounds: dry sand-2000; nitrate soda-20; soda ash-912; lime-100; arsenic-4; uranium-10.

Vaseline Glass Manufacturers

The manufacturers of Vaseline Glass are numerous, and whether or not a particular manufacturer made it depends on which history of glassware you read. While small amounts of Vaseline Glass that are believed to be centuries old have been located, most glassware historians believe that the current process for producing Vaseline Glass began in the mid-1800s, but was not perfected until the 1880s-1890s.

The list of older companies that produced Vaseline Glass reads like the Who's Who in the glassware manufacturing business. They include: Adams & Company; Alexander J. Beatty & Sons; Belmont Glass; Boston & Sandwich Glass, John Bryce & Co.; Cambridge; Central Glass Works; Challinor, Taylor & Co.; Consolidated Lamp Co.; Doyle & Co.; Dugan; Duncan & Sons; Duncan & Miller; Fenton Art Glass; Fostoria; George Davidson & Co.; Gillinder & Sons; Heisey; Hobbs, Brockunier Glass Co.; Imperial; Jefferson Glass Co.; King & Co.; Libbey; McKee; Millersburg Glass; Model Flint Glass; National Glass; Nickel-Plate Glass; Northwood; Pairpoint; Richards & Hartley; Riverside Glass; Stevens & Williams; U. S. Glass; Val St. Lambert; and Westmoreland among others.

Some of the newer companies are Boyd Art Glass; Degenhart; Gibson Glass; Mosser Glass; Summit Art Glass; Viking; Wheaton; and L. G. Wright.

A great deal of detailed historical information on the older glass companies is available to readers via the Internet and in other well-researched publications. Therefore, this author chooses to share information related to several companies and individuals who are currently producing Vaseline Glass. During a lecture in Tulsa, Oklahoma, Bruce Schiwitz provided the following information on Summit Art Glass, Mosser Glass, Gibson Glass, Guernsey Glass and Weishar Enterprises and Island Mold.

Summit Art Glass produces glass in a variety of colors, but works in only one color at a time. They have produced both Vaseline and Vaseline Carnival numerous times and most likely will continue to make runs of it in the future. Summit has some molds that were made exclusively for them. However, the majority of the Summit-owned molds are molds from other glass companies now out of business. Many of the Summit produced wares still carry the marks of the original makers. This is especially true of the Westmoreland and Imperial molds. Some of Summit's glassware is marked with a V in a circle, but markings are not consistent. Identical pieces can be found produced by Summit, one will be marked and the other will not. Summit also does a great deal of contract work for other companies, dealers, private individuals, and clubs. Some of this work is done from Summit molds and some is done from molds owned or provided by the purchasers.

Mosser Glass is one of the larger glassmakers in North America currently batching and producing Vaseline Glass. They produce their own lines as well as do contract and private work for other glass companies, wholesalers, and individuals. Some of these are Rosso, Guernsey, The Degenhart Museum, Weishar, and Fenton, even though Fenton produces their own Vaseline Glass. Mosser has produced Vaseline, Vaseline Carnival, and Vaseline Opalescent. Some of their pieces have been satinized. The majority of Mosser's pieces are marked with an "M" or an "M" in the Ohio outline. Contract pieces are produced to the specifications of the ordering party. In some cases this may result in the piece being produced with an original mold mark or possibly no mark. This practice varies from company to company and is influenced by market trends. Many of the items in Mosser's own line are available from other wholesalers who purchase pieces from Mosser for resale.

Gibson Glass produces a wide variety of blown, mold-blown, and hand crafted glass items. Best known for their glass cruets, they also do a wide range of figurines, vases, perfume bottles, decanters, paperweights, bowls, ring holders, cuspidors, baskets, toothpick holders, oil candles (lamps), and water sets (full and miniature). Gibson has produced Vaseline numerous times. Variety is the spice of life at Gibson and they are ever innovative. A single mold can be fashioned into countless different pieces. A piece can be found in various finishes such as plain, opalescent, carnival, crackle, or a combination of several of these treatments. Gibson works from cullet and normally obtains this from Fenton. In recent years they have produced Vaseline Glass once a year. Most of Gibson's wares are marked with a circular imprint that reads "GIBSON" and the year of production. However, not all molds and pieces have a spot suitable for marking. Also, Gibson will produce goods both in their regular line and special orders without a mark if so requested. Production runs at Gibson are remarkably small and the pieces are quite limited. They may produce a gross of a single style. By comparison, Fenton may produce 2500 of a single piece and consider it "limited." Larger pieces and sets rarely number over a dozen produced within a single year and are very seldom repeated. They also do "experiments" that will usually be marked. The piece may be produced in years to come, but the original experimental piece with the date will be rare, as normally less than a handful are made and sometimes only one.

Guernsey Glass, owned and operated by Harold Bennett, does not actually produce glass. They own the molds and have the pieces produced for them. In recent years, Mosser has produced a great deal of glass for Guernsey Glass. Not all pieces are marked, but some pieces carry a "B" in a triangle outline. Dealers and collectors sometimes mistakenly attribute these pieces to

Boyd. Many Guernsey pieces are from old Cambridge molds, which Bennett owns.

Weishar Enterprises and *Island Mould*, headed by Tom and John Weishar, currently produce most Moon & Star pattern pieces in the marketplace. Mosser and L. E. Smith press these pieces for them in very limited quantities per color. Normally only 75-300 pieces are made in a single color. Some of the molds used are the ones made by Joe Weishar for L. G. Wright. Other molds are newer creations. Most of the pieces carry the "Weishar" signature mark. Several pieces and sets have been produced in Vaseline and Vaseline Carnival.

The Boyd Art Glass Company is a family business that presently produces collectible, affordable novelties. The Boyds worked for Elizabeth Degenhart and purchased the Degenhart factory after her death in 1978. All of Boyd's glass is pressed by hand. The collector can date Boyd glass by the Diamond B logo. Every five years the logo changes: 1978-1983, B inside Diamond; 1983-1988, B inside diamond with horizontal line underneath; 1988-1993, B inside diamond with horizontal line above and below; 1993-1998, B inside diamond with horizontal line above and below and a vertical line on the right; 1998-2003, B inside diamond with horizontal line above and below and a vertical line on the right and left. Boyd glass is unique in that many of its molds are named for family members or close friends. Boyd originally called its Vaseline colored glass Firefly in 1980. In 1988, they issued the color using the names Vaseline and Vaseline Carnival.

Ron Lukian of Rawdon, Quebec, Canada is an independent glass blower. His Vaseline pieces are primarily opalescent and are made from cullet. His specialty is perfume bottles with long daubers. This is something not normally seen in newer productions. He has also produced vases, stemmed goblets, and ring holders. His work is signed and dated (etched) on the bottom and can be found in galleries as well as on eBay.com and other Internet sites.

James Whitehurst is a young, extremely creative, independent glassblower from Cusseta, Georgia. He focuses on artistic glass made from cullet in a combination of Vaseline and other colors. His creations are sold on eBay.com.

As with many other products that were produced in the United States between 1880 and 1920, manufacturers were appealing to rapidly changing tastes within the buying public. Witness the dramatic change in furniture taste—from the dark colors of the Victorian Era, to the appeal of Oak during the Golden Oak Period, to the stark simplicity of the Mission Styles, to the flowery styles of the Art Deco Period. Taste in glassware followed similar trends. One company might produce a style of Vaseline Glass that would be rapidly absorbed by the buying public, only to have second issues of the same design end up in stockpiles on company warehouse shelves.

By the early 1900s, the interest in Vaseline Glass had waned. A few companies attempted to revitalize the interest during the Art Deco Period with small success. However, the unique characteristic of this glass has again captured the interest of collectors and the popularity of Vaseline Glass is once again on the rise.

Vaseline Glass Patterns

Vaseline Glass has been made in many different patterns and shapes. Daisy & Button is the most common, and almost all of the glass companies produced this pattern. Following are some of the patterns and shapes found in this book: Alaska, Bag Ware, Belmont's #100, Brideshead, Cane, Carnelian (Everglades), Coinspot, Coral, Dahlia, Daisy & Button, Daisy & Button with Crossbar (Mikado), Daisy & Button with V Ornament, Daisy & Button with Thumbprint, Daisy & Fern, Dew Drop, Dewey, Diamond Quilted, Diamond Spearhead, Hartley, Heirloom, Hobnail with Thumbprint, Intaglio, Inverted Thumbprint, Lady Caroline, Lattice and Thumbprint, Leaf Mold, Linking Rings, Lords & Ladies, Manila (Wreath and Shell), Maple Leaf, Medallion, Mitered Diamond, Nautilus (Argonaut Shell), Opal Open (Beaded Panels), Petticoats, Polka Dot, Pressed Diamond, Prince William, Queens, Quilted Daisy, Quilted Pillow Sham, Reticulated Cord, Reverse Swirl, Ribbed Spiral, Rose (Rose-in-Snow), Spanish Lace (Opaline Brocade), Swag With Brackets, Swirling Maze, Thousand Eye, Three Panel, Valencia Waffle, Victoria & Albert, War of Roses, William & Mary.

I expended a great deal of time and effort identifying the various patterns in this book. However, I was unable to identify all pieces. If a reader might assist with identification, it would be appreciated. Write to me in care of Schiffer Publishing, Ltd.

Reproductions

Vaseline Glass is no exception when it comes to having reproductions on the market. However, because of its scarcity, all Vaseline Glass is collectible; the difference is in the cost. Following the initial surge of interest in Vaseline Glass and other colored glassware between 1890 and 1930, many manufacturers of glassware began to reproduce some of the more popular pieces. The manufacture of glass was becoming easier and less costly than in the years prior to the 1930s. Many manufacturers decided to "cash in" on the interest in art glass. When old glass companies closed, new glass companies would purchase their molds. Sometimes the original mold was used for the reproduction. Other times, slight variations would be made in the mold. There was a surge of Vaseline

Glass production in the late 1950s to mid-1970s, again in the 1990s, and presently in the 2000s. Some of this production was from new molds, some was reissue of molds that had never been made in Vaseline, and some was/is actual reproductions of molds originally made in Vaseline. Most of the American glass companies producing Vaseline reproductions today (Fenton, Boyd, Summit, Mosser) have marked their glass in a manner that allows collectors to distinguish new versions from the original productions. But, there are exceptions! It would serve the buyer well to study the different patterns and shapes of Vaseline Glass found in this book. Often the sellers themselves do not know the difference between the original design and a reproduction, but the difference in price can be substantial. Be careful to consider shape and pattern along with studying a picture of original glass, so that an expensive error may be avoided.

A simple glance at a picture without also examining the shape and pattern can sometimes be costly.

Vaseline Glass Collectors, Inc.

Incorporated in 1998, Vaseline Glass Collectors, Inc. (VGCI) is a collectors' club dedicated to educating and unifying Vaseline Glass collectors everywhere. The club holds an annual convention and publishes a newsletter six times a year. The author and the photographer of this book are charter members of VGCI and encourage other Vaseline Glass enthusiasts to consider joining as well. Interested readers can obtain information about the club at its homepage, www.vaselineglass.org.

The following abbreviations are used in the captions that follow:

b-base
d-diameter
ea-each
h-height
l-length
nos-not original stopper
pr-pair
sq-square
TP-toothpick
w-width

Chapter II
The Mid-1800s to the Early 1900s

Rubina Verde opalescent *Dew Drop* #5 jug and tumbler by Hobbs, Brockunier & Co., c. 1886. Jug, 7.75"h x 7"d. $450-500. Tumbler, 3.75"h x 2.65"d. $100-150. *Courtesy of Kelvin Russell and Debra Jennings.*

Leaf Mold water pitcher by The Northwood Glass Co., c. 1891. This satin finish *Leaf Mold* pitcher is in red spatter canary. 7.75"h. $600-750. *Collection of Frank, Melissa, & Laura Keathley "Top Shelf Antiques."*

12 The Mid-1800s to the Early 1900s

Carnelian (Everglades) berry set by H. Northwood Co., Wheeling, West Virginia, c. 1903. Master berry bowl, 5.25"h x 10.25"l x 7.75"w. $195-225. Small berry bowl, 2.5"h x 5.3"l x 4.3"w. $50-60 ea. *Courtesy of Dennis & Marilyn Tuttle.*

Petal and Loop candlesticks by Boston and Sandwich Glass, c. 1835-1840. 7"h x 4.25"b. $625-700. *Courtesy of Catherine F. Conrady.*

A Rubina Verde *Polka Dot* cheese and cover by Hobbs, Brockunier & Co., c. 1884. The Hobbs No. 101 Daisy & Button 7" plate is the plate for this cheese dish. 5"h x 7"d. $275-325. *Courtesy of Catherine F. Conrady.*

Spanish Lace (Opaline Brocade) butter dish made by Northwood Co., National Glass Co., and Dugan Glass Co., Indiana, Pennsylvania, c. 1899-1908. *Opaline Brocade* was the original name of the pattern popularly called *Spanish Lace*. This covered butter measures 5.5"h x 8.25"d. $375-425. *Courtesy of Catherine F. Conrady.*

14 The Mid-1800s to the Early 1900s

A Spanish Lace rose bowl and sugar shaker. Rose bowl, 3.75"h x 4.25"d. $70-90. Sugar shaker, 4.5"h x 3.2"d. $125-175. *Courtesy of Catherine F. Conrady.*

Spanish Lace salt and pepper shakers. 2.95"h x 1.5"d. $175-200 pr. *Courtesy of Catherine F. Conrady.*

A *Spanish Lace* celery vase. 6.25"h x 4"d. $125-175. *Courtesy of Catherine F. Conrady.*

Spanish Lace finger bowl on the left, 2.75"h x 4.5"d. $70-90. A *Polka Dot* finger bowl on the right, made by Hobbs, Brockunier & Co. c. 1884. 2.75"h x 5"d. $55-75. *Courtesy of Cindy and Ben Burchfield.*

The Mid-1800s to the Early 1900s 15

Rubina Verde *Polka Dot* cruet No. 308 with original stopper by Hobbs, Brockunier & Co., c. 1884. 6.5"h x 3.7"d. $275-300. *Courtesy of Kelvin Russell and Debra Jennings.*

Daffodils canary opalescent pitcher by H. Northwood Co., Wheeling, West Virginia, c. 1903. Notice the gold trim around the opalescent design and the gold hand painted spider. A very unusual piece. 7"h x 5"d. $825-875. *Courtesy of Kelvin Russell and Debra Jennings.*

16   The Mid-1800s to the Early 1900s

Blown Twist canary opalescent sugar shaker by Northwood & West Virginia Glass, c. 1892-1905. 4.8"h x 3.2"d. $250-350. *Courtesy of Kelvin Russell and Debra Jennings.*

Daffodils vase by H. Northwood Co., Wheeling, West Virginia, c. 1903. This canary opalescent vase has clear feet. 11.25"h. $325-375. *Courtesy of Kelvin Russell and Debra Jennings.*

Stripe Optic canary opalescent bowl by Jefferson Glass Co., c. 1902. 3.75"h x 6.75"d. $75-95. *Courtesy of Kelvin Russell and Debra Jennings.*

The Mid-1800s to the Early 1900s 17

Swirl tumblers: *Reverse Swirl* canary opalescent tumbler by Buckeye Glass Co., c. 1888 and Model Flint Glass Co., 1899. 3.75"h x 2.65"d. $75-95. *Opalescent Swirl* canary tumbler by Jefferson Glass Co., c. 1908. 3.95"h x 2.9"d. $65-75. *Courtesy of Kelvin Russell and Debra Jennings.*

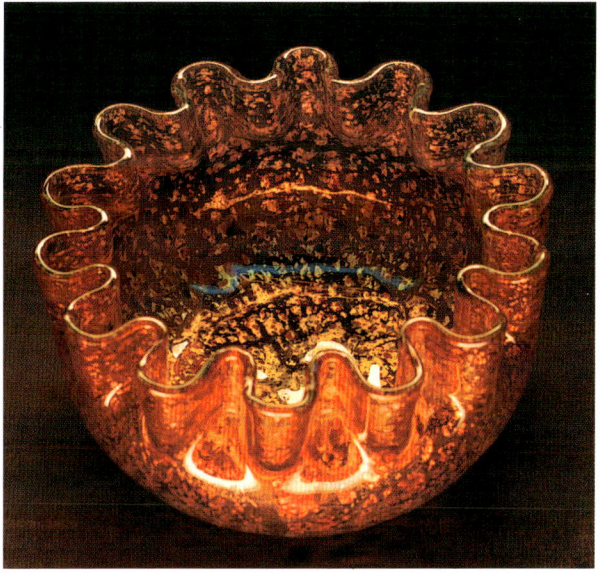

A spangled bowl, red base color with Vaseline plating. There are gold, orange, and blue flecks. This bowl was taken with more fluorescent light than black light so that the colors of the bowl can be seen. With more black light the whole bowl fluoresces green. Maker: possibly Hobbs, Brockunier & Co., c. 1880s. 2.35"h x 4.75"d. $150-200. *Courtesy of Melanie Schonier.*

Stripe opalescent cranberry creamer with canary handle by Northwood Glass Co. and several other companies, c. 1889-1891. 3.65"h x 3.15"d. $140-160. *Courtesy of Kelvin Russell and Debra Jennings.*

Pressed Diamond bride's basket insert by Central Glass Co. c. 1885; U.S. Glass Co. Factory "O", c. 1891. 3"h x 8"sq. The quadruple plate holder is marked Atkinson Silver Co. 11.25"h. $475-525. *Courtesy of Beverly Scherer.*

A Heavy Finecut mustard. The quadruple plate underplate is stamped Simpson Hall Miller & Co. c. 1890s. 5.25"h x 7"d. $150-200. *Courtesy of Beverly Scherer.*

Maple Leaf bride's basket by Gillinder and Sons, c.1885. 3.75"h x 9.75"l x 6.25"w. The stand is marked Pairpoint. 14.25"h x 5.75"l. $275-325.

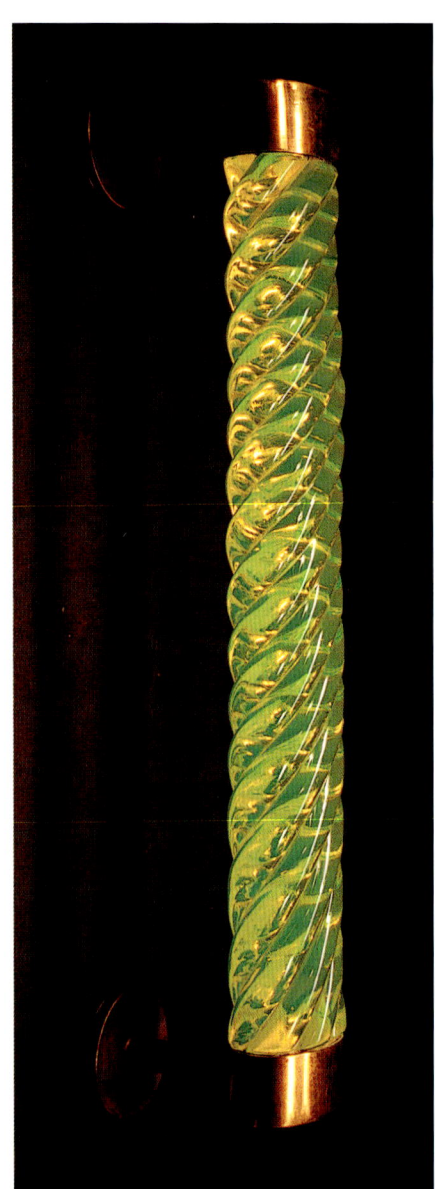

A crystal, Vaseline, rope twist door handle with brass mountings. The owner states that it reportedly came from a hotel or business in New York City area. c. late 1800s. 14"l. $475-525. *Courtesy of Bob and Janet Peper.*

The Mid-1800s to the Early 1900s

The maker of the *Daisy and Button* insert of this pickle castor is unknown. The silver-plated stand is marked Rogers Smith & Co., c. 1880s. 11.25"h. $475-500. *Courtesy of Melanie Schonier*.

Pressed Diamond pickle castor by Central Glass Co., c. 1885, and U.S. Glass Co., c. 1891. The frame has Meriden Silver Plate Co. Quadruple Plate with a lion on the bottom. 11.75"h. $400-450. *Courtesy of Catherine F. Conrady*.

Daisy and Button double pickle castor, maker of inserts unknown. Meriden made the figural quadruple plated frame with bird-foot tongs. c. 1880s. Inserts, 4.12"h x 3.12"d. $550-650. *Courtesy of Melanie Schonier*.

Four bottle castor set with glass holder, maker unknown, c. 1880s. These bottles have an alternating daisy and solid stripe pattern. The holder is clear with a ribbed pattern and X on each side. 10"h x 5.5"sq. $275-300. *Courtesy of Ben Curtis*.

Leaf Mold sugar shaker by The Northwood Glass Co., c. 1891. This pattern is shown here in red spatter canary. 3.75"h x 3.58"d. $425-475.

A *Daisy & Button* condiment set with zinc lids and a glass holder. Maker possibly U.S. Glass, c. 1880-90s. 7"h x 4"d. $150-200. *Courtesy of Catherine F. Conrady.*

Daisy & Button with V Ornament salt shaker by A. J. Beatty & Co., Steubenville, Ohio, c. 1886-1887 and reissued by United States Glass Co., Pittsburgh, Pennsylvania, c. 1892. This pattern has not been reproduced. The shaker has the original zinc lid and lying in front is a mixer that goes in the shaker to keep the salt from solidifying. Unusual to find this mixer with the shaker. $85-95. *Courtesy of Ben Curtis.*

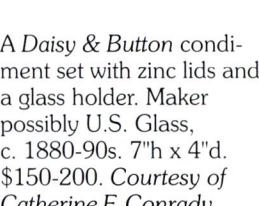

Daisy & Button with V Ornament pickle castor by A. J. Beatty & Co., c. 1886-1887 and reissued by U. S. Glass Co., c. 1892. 4.5"h x 3.1"d. Meriden B. Company made the silver-plated frame. $350-375. *Courtesy of Ben Curtis.*

Stove salt shaker, maker unknown, c. 1880s. $145-165. *Courtesy of Catherine F. Conrady.*

Daisy & Button umbrella match holder by George Duncan & Sons, Factory D of U. S. Glass Co., c. 1892. This little umbrella hung from the oil lamps. 4.65"l x 3.4"d. $75-95. *Courtesy of Catherine F. Conrady.*

Daisy & Button Double Crossroads oil lamp. c. 1870s. The lamp is 10.5"h, the font is 5.5"d, and the cast iron base is 4.6"d. $450-500.

This all glass 1880s oil lamp has EAGLE made in USA P.& A. MFG. Co (Plume and Atwood Manufacturing Co.) embossed on the thumb wheel. 9"h, font 5.7"d. $450-500. *Courtesy of Catherine F. Conrady.*

Bradley & Hubbard oil lamp with a Rubina Verde opalescent *Dew Drop* #1708 globe by Hobbs, Brockunier & Co., c. 1886. Lamp, 27.9"h. Globe, 6.5"h x 9.5"d. $400-500. *Courtesy of Kelvin Russell and Debra Jennings.*

An all glass 1880s oil lamp with hand painted flower and leaf decoration. 14.5"h x 6.25"b, the font is 5.75"d. $450-500. *Courtesy of Catherine F. Conrady.*

A gas light with a *Reverse Swirl* canary cylinder globe in a wrought iron frame. The globe measures 9"h x 7"d, the top is 12"d. Maker unknown, c. late 1880s-1890s. The 1890s are known as the Gas Light Era. The top attaches with screws to the wrought iron frame, is vented, and a fixture at the top (not shown) attaches to the house. $325-375. *Courtesy of Catherine F. Conrady.*

The Mid-1800s to the Early 1900s 23

Dew Drop No. 323 berry set with ground pontil by Hobbs, Brockunier and Co., c. 1886. Master berry, 8"sq. $100-150. Nappy, 4.5"sq. $30-50 ea. *Courtesy of Melanie Schonier.*

Dew Drop No. 323 spooner and celery. Spooner on left, 4"h x 4.25"d. $120-140. Celery on right, 6.5"h x 4"d. $140-160. *Courtesy of Catherine F. Conrady.*

Dew Drop (Hobbs Hobnail) tumblers by Hobbs, Brockunier & Co., c. 1886. Alabaster on the right, 3.8"h x 2.65"d; clear on the left, 3.95"h x 2.65"d. $55-65 ea.. *Courtesy of Catherine F. Conrady.*

24 The Mid-1800s to the Early 1900s

Dew Drop No. 323 (Hobbs Hobnail) toothpick. 2.3"h x 1.75"d. $55-65. *Courtesy of Catherine F. Conrady.*

Dew Drop No. 323 cruet. 7.5"h x 4"d. $275-325. *Courtesy of Catherine F. Conrady.*

Diamond Spearhead berry set by Northwood Glass Co., c. 1901. Master berry, 3"h x 9"d. $175-200. Small berry, 1.5"h x 4"d. $40-60 ea.

The Mid-1800s to the Early 1900s 25

Diamond Spearhead covered butter. 5.25"h x 7.5"d. $450-500.

Diamond Spearhead tumblers. 3.75"h. $80-100 ea.

An *Alaska* banana boat by The Northwood Glass Co. c. 1897. This pattern is very collectible. It is sometimes decorated with enameled forget-me-not flowers and elephant ear leaves, with or without gold. This decorated piece is 2.75"h x 9.75"l x 6"w. $250-325. *Courtesy of Catherine F. Conrady.*

No. 101 Daisy & Button Star berry set by Hobbs, Brockunier & Co. c. 1884. The pair of smooth grooves in each corner that meet in the bottom identify this set as Hobbs (see Bredehoft's *Hobbs, Brockunier & Co., Glass*, pg.74). Master berry, 3"h x 9"d. $125-150. Nappy, 1.5"h x 5"d. $25-50 ea. *Courtesy of Catherine F. Conrady.*

Rose (Rose-in-Snow) berry set. This berry set is pictured in Heacock's *U. S. Glass from A to Z* in a reprint ad from Factory E, c. 1891. The flower design alternates panels. The view in this photo matches the small bowl in the ad. The ad reads 9" Rose berry dish and 5" Rose berry dish. Master berry, 3"h x 9"sq. $75-100. Small berry, 1.75"h x 5"sq. $20-30 ea. *Courtesy of Catherine F. Conrady.*

Ribbed Spiral bon bon by Model Flint Glass Co., c. 1899-1902. This ruffled bowl is 2.75"h x 6.75"d. $65-85. *Courtesy of Catherine F. Conrady*

The Mid-1800s to the Early 1900s 27

Coral bowl attributed to Jefferson Glass Co. by Heacock based on color and pattern characteristics. probably c. late 1800s to early 1900s. 2.35"h x 8.75"d. $50-65. *Courtesy of Catherine F. Conrady.*

Swirling Maze bowl by Jefferson Glass Co., c. 1905. 10"d. $175-200. *Courtesy of Cindy and Ben Burchfield.*

Coinspot bowl. Several of the early glass companies made this pattern from the late 1800s to the early 1900s (Belmont Glass Co., c. 1887; Hobbs, c. 1888; Northwood, c. 1890; Beaumont Glass Co., c. 1900; Dugan Glass Co., c. 1904; Fenton Art Glass Co., c. 1907). 3.75"h x 10"l x 7"w. $75-100. *Courtesy of Catherine F. Conrady.*

Hobnail and Paneled Thumbprint bowls by H. Northwood Co., Wheeling, West Virginia, c. 1905. 1.75"h x 4.7"d. $60-75. *Courtesy of Catherine F. Conrady.*

This 9" Vaseline bowl has a draped pattern with an edge treatment in speckled cranberry. Possibly Jefferson, c. late 1800s. $180-225. *Courtesy of Cindy and Ben Burchfield.*

28 The Mid-1800s to the Early 1900s

Lattice and Daisy tumbler by Dugan Glass, c. 1914. This pattern was made mainly in Carnival glass and is considered scarce in Vaseline. 4.25"h x 2.8"d. $120-130.

Intaglio jelly compote by The Northwood Glass Co., c. 1897. This pattern has not been reproduced. 4.5"h x 4.65"d. $75-95.

Swag with Brackets creamer and sugar by Jefferson Glass Co., c. 1904. The creamer is 4.6"h x 3.87"d. $80-100. The covered sugar is 6.75"h x 4.12"d. $120-130.

Nautilus (Argonaut Shell) creamer by The Northwood Glass Co. and Dugan Glass Co., c. 1898-1910. 4.5"h x 4.5"l x 3.3"w. $100-125. *Courtesy of Catherine F. Conrady.*

The Mid-1800s to the Early 1900s 29

Manila (Wreath and Shell) spooner by Model Flint Glass Co., Albany, Indiana, c. 1899-1903. 4.5"h x 3.6"d. $125-150. *Courtesy of Catherine F. Conrady.*

Dahlia water pitcher by Canton Glass Company, Canton, Ohio, c. 1880s. 8.25"h. $125-150. *Courtesy of Catherine F. Conrady.*

Medallion water pitcher, maker unknown, c. 1885-1895. This pattern is also known as *Spades* and *Hearts and Spades*. 9.25"h. $150-200. *Courtesy of Catherine F. Conrady.*

Daisy & Button bulbous pitcher, possibly by Bryce Brothers that became Factory B of U. S. Glass Co., c. 1890s. Bryce's *Daisy and Button* pattern was originally called *Fashion*. 7.75"h x 6"d. $150-175. *Courtesy of Cindy and Ben Burchfield.*

The pattern of this water pitcher closely resembles *Triple Bar (Scalloped Prism)* by Doyle and Co. #84, c. 1880s and U. S. Glass Co., c. 1895. However, McCain only references crystal in her book. 7.75"h x 4.8"d, $200-250. *Courtesy of W. C. "Red" Roetteis.*

Fine Cut and Panel milk pitcher by Bryce Brothers, Pittsburgh, Pennsylvania, and Richards & Hartley Glass Co., Pittsburgh, Pennsylvania, c. 1889. Reissued in early 1890s by U. S. Glass Co. factory B (Bryce Bros.). The original pattern name was *"Russian"* at Hartley and pattern line No. 260 at U. S. Glass. Also known as *Button and Oval Medallion* and *Nailhead and Panel*. 7"h x 4.9"d. $95-125. *Courtesy of W. C. "Red" Roetteis.*

The Mid-1800s to the Early 1900s 31

Fine Cut and Panel compote. 6.75"h x 6.75"d x 5"b. $100-125.

A small single lily epergne. Maker and circa date unknown. Help with identification would be appreciated. 8.75"h x 6.25"d. $75-100. *Courtesy of Catherine F. Conrady.*

Daisy & Button with Thin Bar spooner by U. S. Glass Co. Factory G (Gillinder & Sons), c. 1891. 4.75"h x 3.9"d. $65-85. *Courtesy of Catherine F. Conrady.*

Pattern #100 high standard compote by Belmont Glass Works, c. 1886-1890. 11.25"h x 7.75"d. $300-350. *Courtesy of Catherine F. Conrady.*

32 The Mid-1800s to the Early 1900s

Belmont Pattern #100 covered butter. This pattern is a very fancy form of *Daisy and Button*. 8.5"h x 8"d. $275-325. *Courtesy of Catherine F. Conrady.*

Daisy & Button Crossbar covered, footed butter. 6.5"h x 6.75"d. $200-250.

Daisy & Button Crossbar (Mikado) berry bowl by Richards and Hartley, Tarentum, Pennsylvania, c. 1885. Reissued by U. S. Glass Co. Factory E, c. 1891. 4.5"h x 8.25"d. $75-100. *Courtesy of Linda Wilder.*

Medallion covered butter. Maker unknown, c. 1885-1895. 5.5"h x 6.5"l x 6.5"w. $200-250. *Courtesy of Cindy and Ben Burchfield.*

The Mid-1800s to the Early 1900s 33

Inverted Thumbprint cheese and cover. Maker unknown, c. 1880-90s. The three applied legs, not pictured, are shaped like the finial. The edge of the plate turns up, the edge of the lid is beaded, prunt on base. 7.5"h x 9.75"d. $185-225. *Courtesy of Cindy and Ben Burchfield.*

Group of goblets. Left: *Rose-in-Snow* goblet, Bryce Brothers of Pittsburgh, Pennsylvania, c. 1880s and continued by U. S. Glass Co. after 1891. Reproduced by Summit in 1978 and B & P Lamp Supply Company of McMinnville, Tennessee in 1960. 5.75"h x 3.15"d x 3.2"b. $35-45. Center: *Daisy & Button with Thumbprint*, Adams & Co. of Pittsburgh, Pennsylvania, c. 1886 and continued by U. S. Glass Co. after 1891. Reproduced by L. G. Wright Glass Co., c. 1969. 6.25"h x 3.45"d x 3.15"b. $35-45. Right: *Polka Dot* goblet by Hobbs, Brockunier and Co., c. 1885-1890. 5.75"h x 3"d x 3"b. $35-45. *Courtesy of Catherine F. Conrady.*

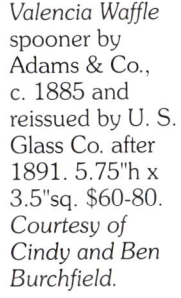

Valencia Waffle spooner by Adams & Co., c. 1885 and reissued by U. S. Glass Co. after 1891. 5.75"h x 3.5"sq. $60-80. *Courtesy of Cindy and Ben Burchfield.*

Mitered Diamond goblet by Jefferson Glass Co., c. 1880s. This pattern is also called *Sunken Buttons and Pyramid*. 6"h x 3.5"d. $50-75. *Courtesy of Cindy and Ben Burchfield.*

Hartley (Panelled Diamond Cut and Fan, U. S. Glass No. 900) by Richards & Hartley Glass Co., c. 1887; reissued by U. S. Glass, c. 1891. This goblet has three clear oval panels with alternate fine cut panels. The fine cut panels have a fan pattern at the top, and the oval panels are outlined with a bead pattern. The glass is very pretty and clear. 5.9"h x 3.25"d x 3.2"b. $60-75.

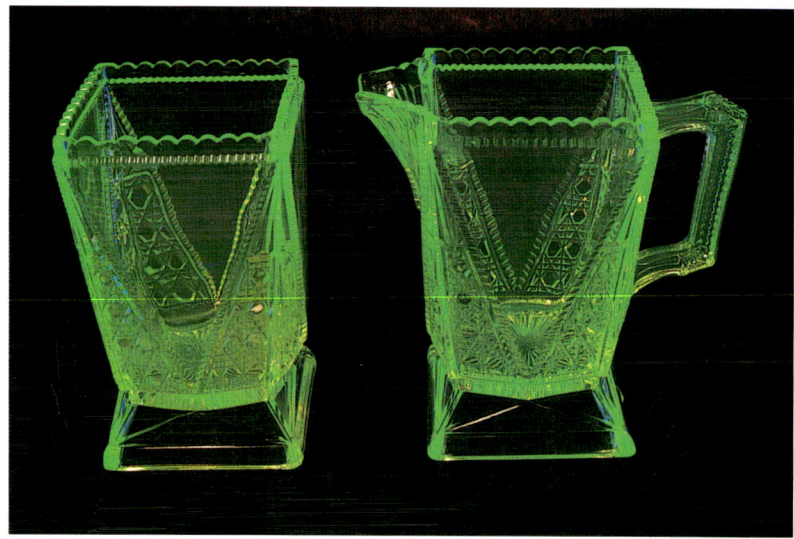

Mitered Diamond creamer and spooner. Creamer, 5.5"h x 3"sq. $65-85. Spooner, 5.25"h x 3.25"sq. $60-80. *Courtesy of Cindy and Ben Burchfield.*

Mitered Diamond sugar bowl. 8"h x 3.75"sq. $125-150. *Courtesy of Cindy and Ben Burchfield.*

Mitered Diamond butter dish. 5.75"h x 6.5"sq. $175-200. *Courtesy of Cindy and Ben Burchfield.*

The Mid-1800s to the Early 1900s 35

Mitered Diamond berry bowl. 2.5"h x 7.5"sq. $75-100. Courtesy of Cindy and Ben Burchfield.

Pressed Diamond low standard open comport. 4.75"h x 7.75"d. $75-100. Courtesy of Catherine F. Conrady.

Pressed Diamond cake stand by Central Glass Co., c. 1885 and reissued by U. S. Glass Co. Factory O (Central Glass), c. 1891. 4.25"h x 9.75"d. $75-100. Courtesy of Catherine F. Conrady.

Pressed Diamond sauce dishes. 1.5"h x 5.25"d. $30-60. Courtesy of Catherine F. Conrady.

36 The Mid-1800s to the Early 1900s

Pressed Diamond table set. Spooner, 4.55"h x 4.35"d. $45-65. Covered sugar bowl, 7.5"h x 4"d. $75-95. Creamer, 4.55"h x 3.5"d. $50-70. *Courtesy of Catherine F. Conrady.*

Bag Ware straight sided celery. 6.6"h x 4.25"d. $75-95. *Courtesy of Catherine F. Conrady.*

Bag Ware Duncan & Sons # 800 covered comport, c. 1885. Continued production by U. S. Glass Co. c. 1891. 7.25"h x 8.25"d. $175-200. *Courtesy of Catherine F. Conrady.*

Bag Ware cruet. According to Heacock, the stopper should match the finial on the covered comport. 6.75"h x 3.6"d. $125-175. *Courtesy of Catherine F. Conrady.*

The Mid-1800s to the Early 1900s   37

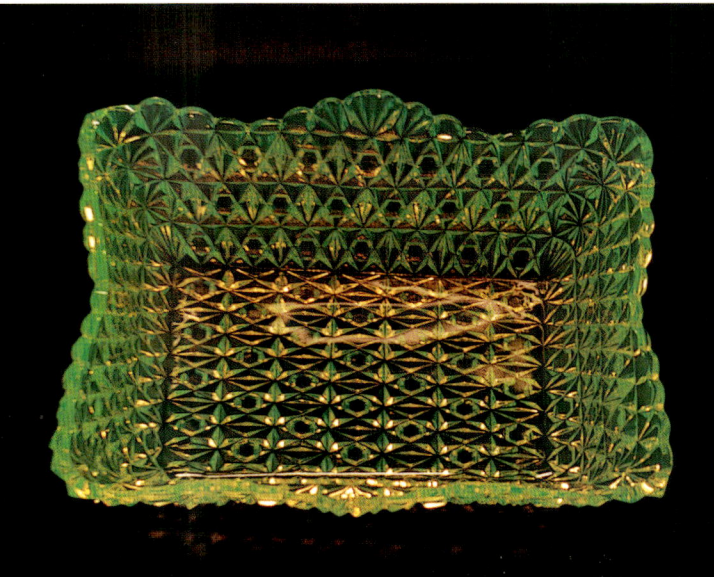

Berry bowl, c. 1890s. The pattern of this large rectangular bowl is very similar to *Pressed Diamond*. However, I did not find this shape bowl listed. Help with identification would be appreciated. $90-120. *Courtesy of Catherine F. Conrady.*

Daisy & Button with Thumbprint tray, possibly by Adams & Co., c. 1886, reissued by U. S. Glass Co., c. 1891. The design of this tray is very sharp and well defined which indicates that it is probably old. Numerous companies produced *Daisy and Button* and variants of the pattern in the late 1800s and it has been reproduced many times since the 1930s. Reproductions are less defined, heavier, and thicker. 15.25"l x 9.75"w. $100-125. *Courtesy of Catherine F. Conrady.*

Flattened Fine Cut sugar. Maker: Possibly U. S. Glass Co., c. 1891. This sugar has horizontal lines on the handle side. 4"h x 3.9"l x 2.6"d. $30-50. *Courtesy of Catherine F. Conrady.*

Three Panel covered sugar and sauces by Richards and Hartley Glass Co., c. 1880s and reissued by U. S. Glass Co. Factory E (Richards and Hartley), c. 1891. Sauce, 2.25"h x 3.6"d. $25-45 ea. Sugar, 7"h x 4"d. $80-100. *Courtesy of Catherine F. Conrady.*

Two Panel salt and pepper shakers by Richards & Hartley Glass Co., early 1880s and continued by U. S. Glass Co. Factory E in 1891. 3.7"h x 1.6"d. $150-175. *Courtesy of Catherine F. Conrady.*

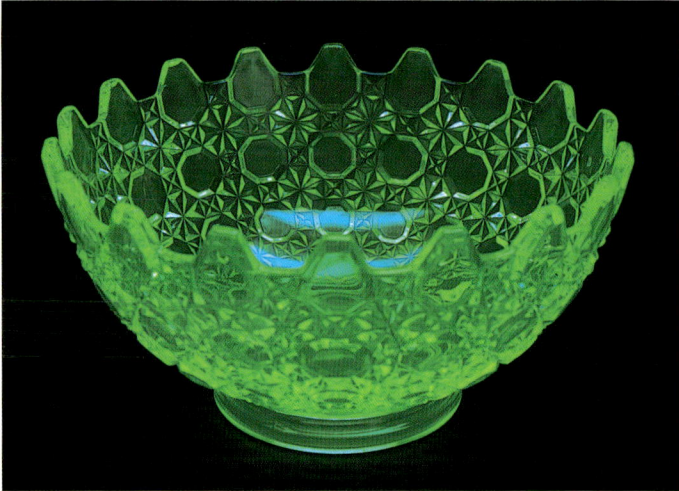

Daisy & Button fruit bowl by U. S. Glass Co., c. 1890s. 4.5"h x 9"d. $125-150. *Courtesy of Linda Wilder.*

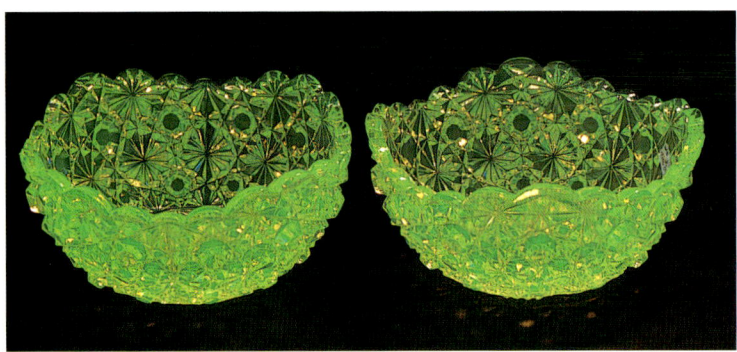

Daisy & Button (Fashion) nappies by U. S. Glass Co. Factory B (Bryce Bros.), c. 1890s. 2.3"h x 4.8"d. $30-50. *Courtesy of Catherine F. Conrady.*

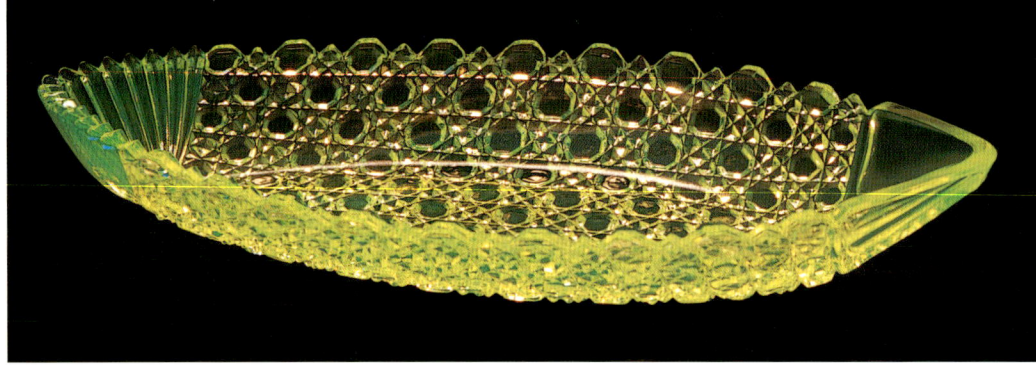

Cane canoe relish dish, possibly by Gillinder & Sons, c. 1885 and McKee Glass Co., c. 1894. Notice that one end is plain and the other has ribbing. 1"h x 7.75"l x 3.5"w. $75-95. *Courtesy of Catherine F. Conrady.*

Daisy & Button canoe celery by George Duncan & Son, c. 1884. 12.75"l x 4.25"w. $100-125. *Courtesy of Melanie Schonier.*

The Mid-1800s to the Early 1900s   39

Lattice and Thumbprint syrup pitcher by Central Glass, c. 1880s. 6"h x 3.15"d. $275-300. Courtesy of Melanie Schonier.

Dewey grouping: Maker; Indiana Tumbler & Goblet Co., c. 1898 and continued production by U. S. Glass Co. until 1904. This pattern was named Dewey to commemorate Admiral Dewey's victories in the Spanish-American War. Back row, left: Table size covered sugar, 4.75"h x 3.75"d. $100-140. Back row, right: Table size butter, 4.5"h x 5"d, $100-140. Front row, left: Spooner, 3.6"h x 3.7"d. $70-90. Front row, right: Frappe (parfait) without lid, 5.75"h x 3.9"d. $75-95. Courtesy of Catherine F. Conrady.

Lattice and Thumbprint spooner.
4.75"h x 3.55"d. $80-100.
Courtesy of Catherine F. Conrady.

40 The Mid-1800s to the Early 1900s

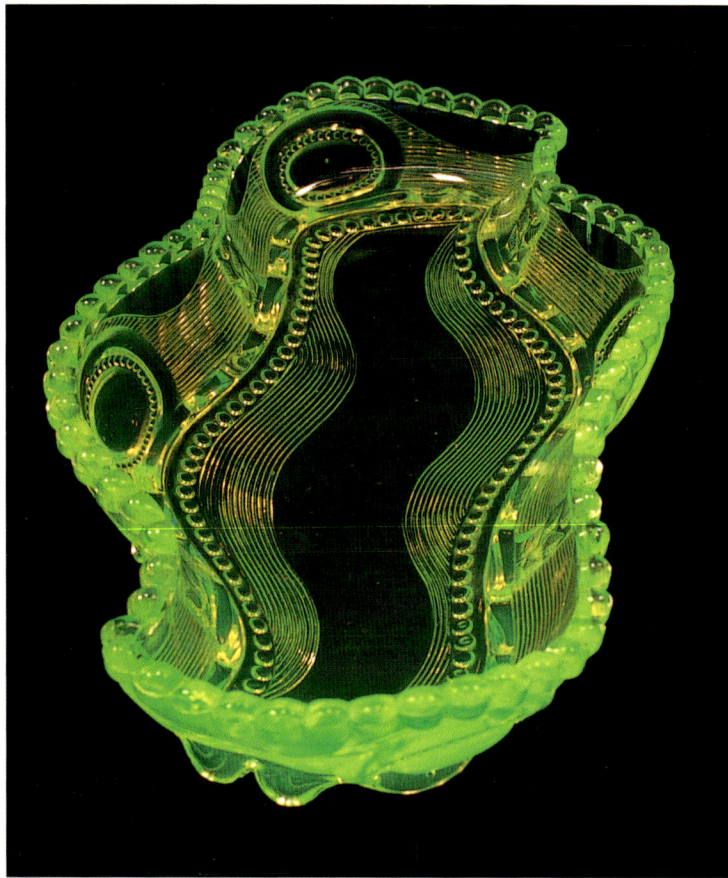

Dewey serpentine shaped tray, 1.9"h x 10.25"l x 5.5"w. $75-95. *Courtesy of Catherine F. Conrady*

Dewey footed master berry bowl, 3.5"h x 8"d. $100-150. *Courtesy of Catherine F. Conrady.*

Quilted Diamond (Diamond Quilted) footed sauce, maker unknown, c. 1880s. 2.5"h x 4.4"d. $30-35 ea. *Courtesy of Catherine F. Conrady.*

Dewey footed plate, 2"h x 7.5"d. $75-95. *Courtesy of Catherine F. Conrady*

Quilted Diamond octagonal plate, 6"d. $20-30. Cordial, 3.8"h x 1.8"d. $40-50. *Courtesy of Catherine F. Conrady.*

The Mid-1800s to the Early 1900s 41

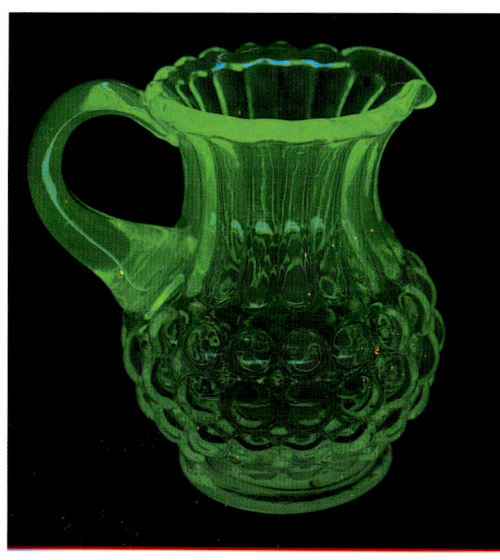

Thousand Eye creamer by Adams & Co., c. 1874; Richards & Hartley Glass Co. # 103, c. 1880; U. S. Glass Co. at Factories A and E, c. 1891. 4.25"h x 3.35"d. $60-70.

Quilted Diamond sauce dish, 1.25"h x 4"d. $20-30.

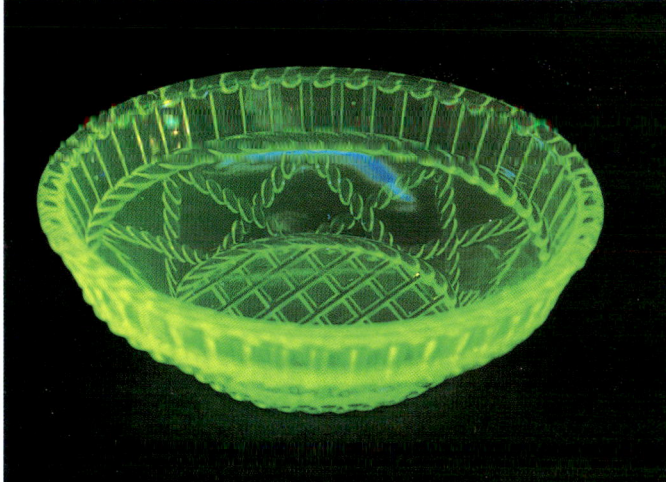

Reticulated Cord sauce bowl by U. S. Glass Co., c. 1891. This pattern is reportedly scarce in color. 1.2"h x 4.4"d. $35-45.

Reticulated Cord creamer. $45-55. *Courtesy of Linda Wilder.*

Queens covered sugar by McKee Glass Co., c. 1894. Mosser has reproduced this pattern in the butter dish, cake stand, compote, and water set. 7.5"h x 4.25"d x 3.4"b. $75-95. *Courtesy of Catherine F. Conrady.*

Banner relish tray by J. B. Higbee Glass Co., c. 1909. This relish dish has the Higbee logo in the bottom (a bee with an H in left wing, an I in body of bee, a G in right wing). 1.75"h x 7"l x 5"w. $50-75. *Courtesy of Catherine Conrady.*

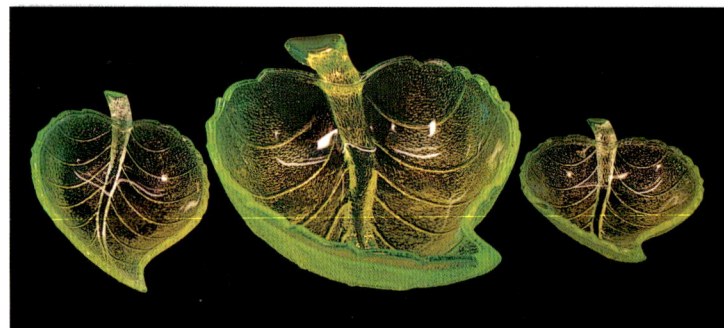

Leaf berry set by Portland Glass Co., c. 1864-1873. Portland No. 1535 Portland Birch Leaf. L. G. Wright has reproduced this pattern. Master berry, 10.5"l x 7.25"d. $50-70. Small berry, 6"l x 4.1"w. $20-30 ea. *Courtesy of Cindy and Ben Burchfield.*

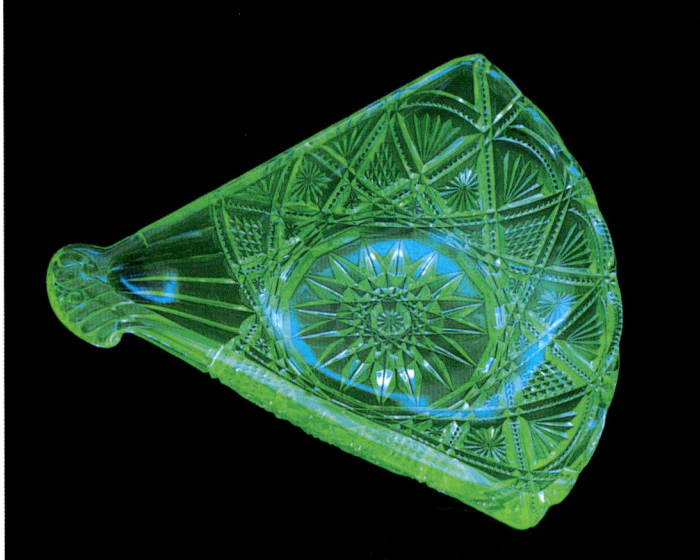

This pressed glass fan is a very good imitation of cut glass. The design is very sharp and the handle is detailed. The color is the light canary of the 1880-90s. Help with identification would be appreciated. 7"l x 6.75"d. $75-100. *Courtesy of Linda Wilder.*

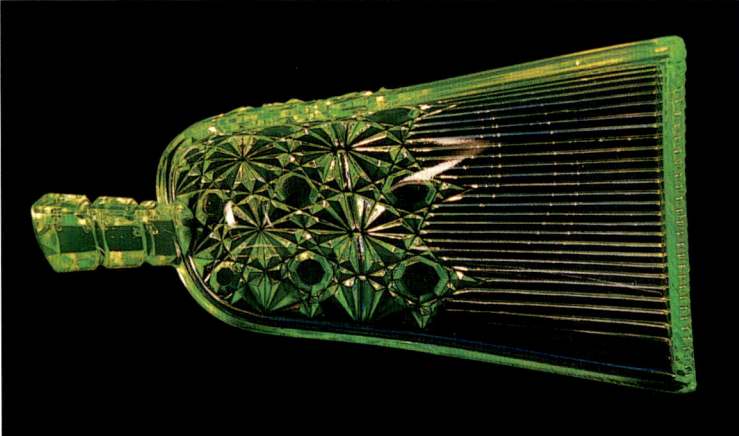

Wiskbroom pickle dish made by Campbell, Jones & Co., c. 1880s, and George Duncan & Sons, c. 1886. $70-80. Recently reproduced by Summit Art Glass, c. 1990s. $20-25. *Courtesy of Catherine F. Conrady.*

Cat toothpick by U. S. Glass Factory E (Richards & Hartley), c. 1892. 3.5"h x 2.5"sq.b. $75-95. *Courtesy of Catherine F. Conrady.*

The Mid-1800s to the Early 1900s   43

Old Oaken Bucket (Wooden Pail, Oaken Bucket) spooner made by Bryce, Higbee & Co., Pittsburgh, Pennsylvania, c. 1880s; reissued by U. S. Glass Co. Factory B after 1891. 4.5"h x 3.25"d. $65-75. *Courtesy of Linda Wilder.*

Sad Iron butter dish originally made by U. S. Glass Co., c. 1890s. 4.5"h x 8.75"l x 5"w. $125-150. Reproduced by L. G. Wright as a *Flat Iron* candy box, c. 1950-60s. $50-55. *Courtesy of Catherine F. Conrady.*

Master Salts by Central Glass, c. 1880. These oval salts have a smooth top half and a ribbed base. 1.6"h x 4"l x 3.1"w. $65-75 ea. *Courtesy of Catherine F. Conrady.*

Petticoat hat toothpick by Riverside Glass Works, c. 1899. The pattern of this Vaseline hat with gold decoration is also known as *National*. 3.37"h x 5.75"l x 5.25"w. $95-110. *Courtesy of Cindy and Ben Burchfield.*

A master *Bird & Berry* salt originally produced by McKee, c. 1890-1900. 2.1"h x 3.9"l. Reproduced by L. G. Wright Glass Co. The reproduction measures 1.8"h x 4"l and the mold detail is less distinct. $40-60. *Courtesy of Catherine F. Conrady.*

44 The Mid-1800s to the Early 1900s

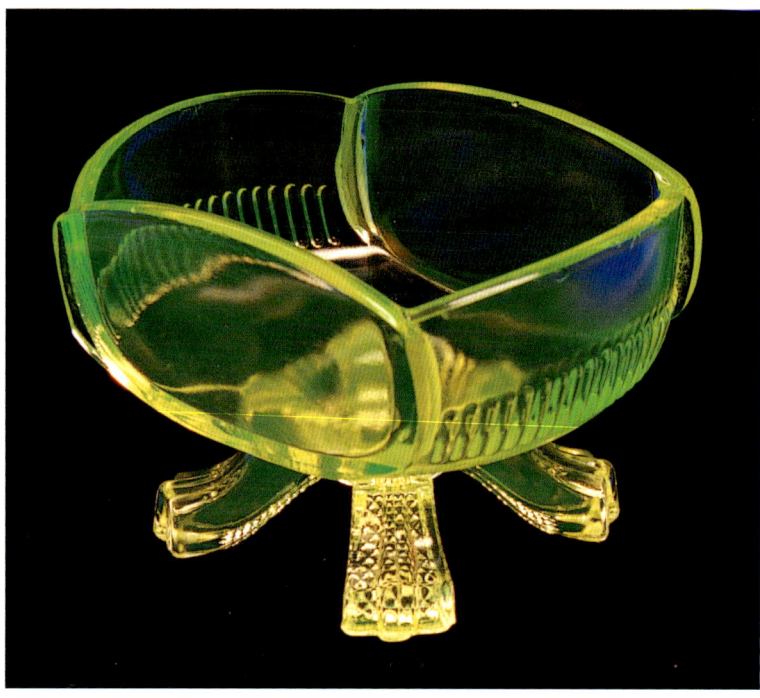

A footed master salt. Maker unknown, c. 1880-90s. 3.90"h x 4.25"l x 3"w. $55-75. *Courtesy of Cindy and Ben Burchfield.*

A large optic, blown Vaseline hat, celery vase size. Maker unknown, c. possibly 1880-90s. 5"h x 6.35"l x 6"w. $70-80. *Courtesy of Catherine F. Conrady.*

Razor sharpener. Maker unknown, c. possibly 1890s. 3"l x 1.5"w. $50-75. *Courtesy of Cindy and Ben Burchfield.*

Coach Bowl by McKee & Bros., c. 1886. Reproduced by L. G. Wright in other colors but not Vaseline according to Red Roetteis. 4.5"h x 8"l x 5.25"w. $100-150. *Courtesy of Catherine F. Conrady.*

Lady's Head paperweight. This commemorative paperweight is mold marked WORLDS FAIR 1893 Libbey Glass Co. Toledo, Ohio. $325-375. *Courtesy of Catherine F. Conrady.*

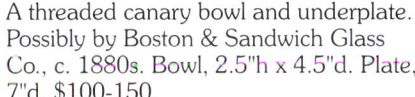

A threaded canary bowl and underplate. Possibly by Boston & Sandwich Glass Co., c. 1880s. Bowl, 2.5"h x 4.5"d. Plate, 7"d. $100-150.

Candlesticks: Left: A spindle shaped candlestick, Imperial #635, c. 1920s. 8.37"h x 4.1"b, $55-60. Right: A heavy candlestick with a metal socket possibly Sandwich, c. mid to late 1800s. 8.25"h x 4.3"b. $125-175. *Courtesy of Catherine F. Conrady.*

A *Jack-in-the-Pulpit* canary vase with opalescent top, c. 1880s. 5.75"h x 3.3"d. $125-150. *Courtesy of Catherine F. Conrady.*

A Victorian 12" Vaseline Mary Gregory vase, c. 1880s. American made Mary Gregory is white while English made is flesh tone. Notice the grave with the cross in the background. $400-600. *Courtesy of Betty and Del Kerr.*

The Mid-1800s to the Early 1900s 47

A *Jack-in-the-Pulpit* canary opalescent striped vase with applied rigaree; embossed with Pan American 1901 with gold decoration. Maker: National Glass Company's Northwood Glass Works, Indiana. 6.5"h x 3.65"d. $125-150. *Courtesy of Catherine F. Conrady.*

Waffle pattern, opalescent, single lily epergne, c. 1880s. The maker of the lily is unknown. The holder has Meriden B Company on the bottom. 11.25"h. $350-400. *Courtesy of Catherine F. Conrady.*

48   The Mid-1800s to the Early 1900s

Tall opalescent ribbed vase. This vase resembles many of the vases made in the early 1900s by Northwood and Dugan. 16.25"h x 4.1"b. $60-80. *Courtesy of Catherine F. Conrady.*

This Victorian vase has an opalescent and cranberry ruffled top, c. 1880-90s. 12"h x 4.25"b. $125-150. *Courtesy of Melanie Schonier.*

Ribbed Spiral 10" vase by Model Flint Glass Co., Albany, Indiana, c. 1899-1902. *Courtesy of Merle Pfannenstiel.*

The Mid-1800s to the Early 1900s 49

Reverse Swirl opalescent rose bowl. Originally made by Buckeye Glass Co. and then by Model Flint Glass Co., c. 1888-1902. John Miller patented this process and worked at both factories. 4.25"h x 5"d. $125-140. *Courtesy of Catherine F. Conrady.*

Hyacinth vase. Vases of this shape are referred to as "bulb pushers" and were popular in the nineteenth century. 6"h x 3.85"b. $80-100. *Courtesy of Catherine F. Conrady.*

A tall candelabra, possibly by Pairpoint, c. early 1900s. 13.75"h x 4.65"b. $175-200. *Courtesy of Catherine F. Conrady.*

Fluted Bars and Beads vase by Jefferson Glass Co., Steubenville, Ohio, c. 1904. This vase can be found with and without cranberry edging and in slightly different forms at the top. 6.89"h x 5"d x 3.1"b. $85-100.

An iridized, pinched vase, possibly by Dugan, c. 1905-07. 4.5"h x 4.3"d. $65-75. *Courtesy of Melanie Schonier.*

Beads and Bark vase by Northwood Glass Co., c. 1903. 6.5"h x 3"d. $100-125.

The Mid-1800s to the Early 1900s 51

Maple Leaf Chalice by Northwood Glass Co., c. 1903. 6.25"h x 3.5"d. $75-95. *Courtesy of Cindy and Ben Burchfield.*

A double handled urn by U. S. Glass Co., c. 1900. 10.5"h x 3.5"sq.b. $125-150. *Courtesy of Catherine F. Conrady.*

A one quart opaque water jug or carafe cased in Vaseline, c. 1890-1900s. 8"h x 4.75"d. $75-95. *Courtesy of Cindy and Ben Burchfield.*

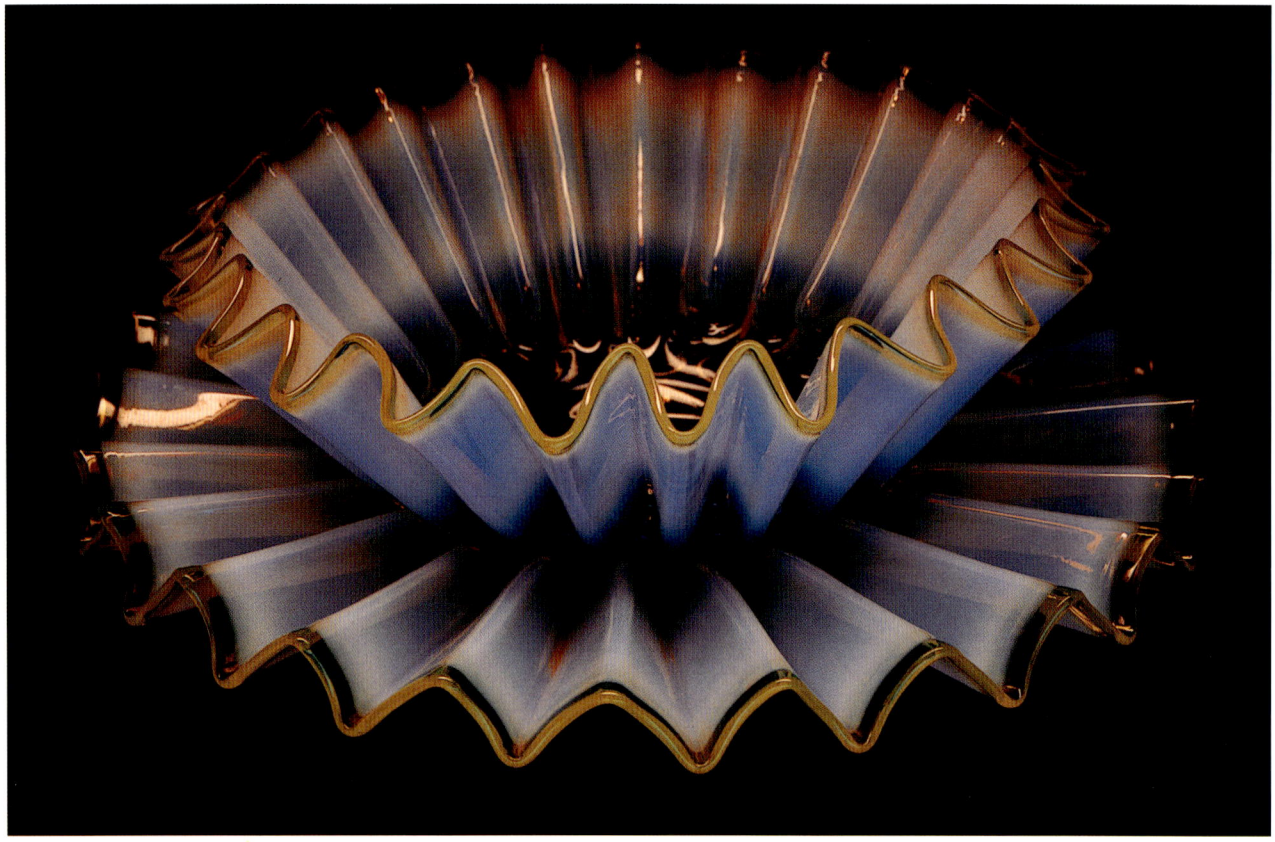

A large opalescent, deeply crimped bowl and matching underplate with Vaseline rim and ground and polished pontil similar to styles of the 1880s. Bowl, 4.25"h x 10"d. Plate, 2.25"h x 13"d. $200-250. *Courtesy of Melanie Schonier.*

A magnificent Victorian 11.5" bride's bowl in original numbered Pairpoint stand. This white *Dew Drop* bowl is cased with cranberry on the inside and Vaseline on the outside. Hobbs, Brockunier & Co., c. 1886. $1200-1500. *Courtesy of Betty and Del Kerr.*

Chapter III
The 1920s to the 1940s

L. G. Wright's Vaseline opalescent epergne with crystal crest on cones, c. 1940s. Red Roetteis and James Measell furnish the following information in their book *The L. G. Wright Glass Company*: Joe Weishar's Island Mould and Machine Co. made the molds for L. G. Wright's large pressed epergne in the early 1940s. The epergne consists of a large central cone and three smaller cones, mounted in a glass fitting attached with a metal peg to the large base. Harry Northwood's No. 305 Flower Stand was the inspiration for this epergne. 17"h x 10"d. $1000-1100. *Courtesy of Catherine F. Conrady.*

A Vaseline Glass fish bowl, c. 1937. 8.5"h x 13.75"d. $140-160. *Courtesy of Catherine F. Conrady.*

54   The 1920s to the 1940s

Tiffin pattern No. 310 pedestal flared bowl, c. 1920s. 5"h x 9"d x 4.5"b. $65-85. Courtesy of Catherine F. Conrady.

Rolled rim satin glass console bowl on black base, possibly by Fenton, c. 1920s. Bowl 3.5"h x 9.75"d. $75-85. Courtesy of Catherine F. Conrady.

Imperial Glass's Golden Green (Vaseline) No. 320 Double Scroll oval console bowl, c. 1920s. 4.35"h x 11"l x 9.25"w. $80-100. Courtesy of Catherine F. Conrady.

No. 314 flared topaz iridized stretch glass console on black base, by U. S. Glass, c. 1920-30s. 3.3"h x 8.3"d. $75-100. Courtesy of Catherine F. Conrady.

The 1920s to the 1940s   55

Topaz sherbets by U. S. Glass, c. 1920-30s. 4.5"h x 3.8"d x 2.7"b. $45-55 ea. *Courtesy of Catherine F. Conrady.*

No. 637 flared stretch glass comport by H. Northwood and Co., c. 1916-25. 7.25"h x 5.5"d x 3.25"b. $75-95 *Courtesy of Catherine F. Conrady.*

Fan Vase No. 847 by Fenton, c. 1921. This melon-rib, topaz iridescent stretch glass fan vase is 4.95"h x 8.75"l x 3.95"w. $75-100. *Courtesy of Catherine F. Conrady.*

No. 310 Open Work canary satin glass compote by Tiffin, c. 1920s. This bowl is pictured on its side for detail. 4.25"h x 12.25"d. $55-75. *Courtesy of Catherine F. Conrady.*

An iridescent stretch plate, possibly by H. Northwood and Co., c. 1916-25. This plate has twenty optic rays and hand painted flowers. 6.5"d. $25-35. *Courtesy of Catherine F. Conrady.*

No. 643 Salver by Fenton Art Glass Company, c. 1920-30s. This iridescent stretch glass salver is 2.75"h. $55-75. *Courtesy of Catherine F. Conrady.*

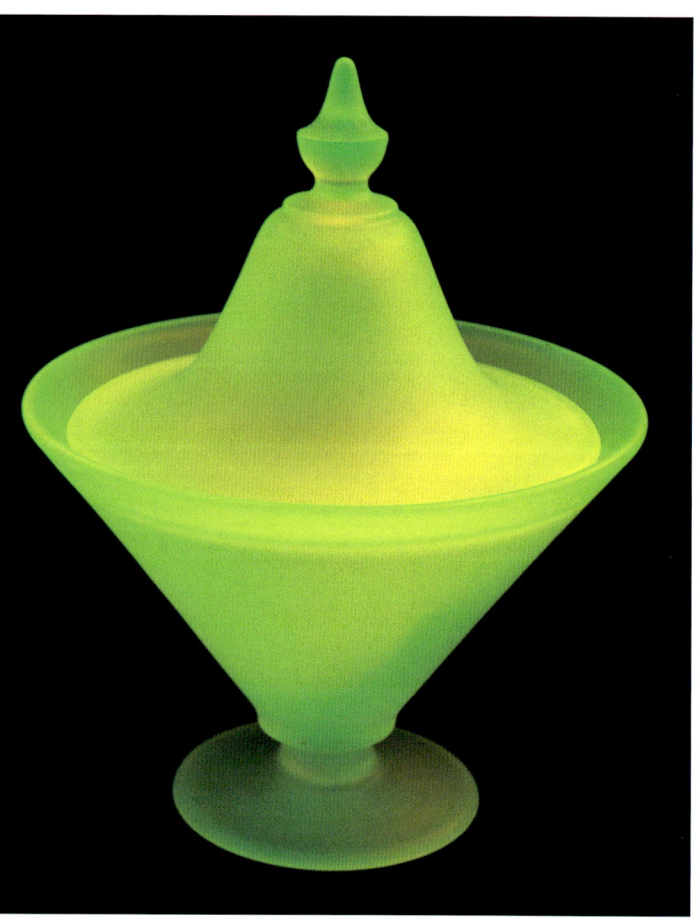

No. 179 satin conic candy box by Tiffin, c. 1920s, 7.75"h x 6.1"d x 3.1"b. $55-75. *Courtesy of Catherine F. Conrady.*

The 1920s to the 1940s 57

A satin glass *Bon Bon* box and cover, possibly by U. S. Glass Co., c. 1926. 3.25"h x 6.25"d. $65-85. *Courtesy of Catherine F. Conrady.*

Faux Crackle "By Cracky" octagon shaped sherbets by L. E. Smith, c. 1926. 3.25"h x 3.5"w x 2.37"b. $30-45 ea. *Courtesy of Catherine F. Conrady.*

Fenton's No. 220 lemonade set, c. 1920s. The covered 76 oz. jug and 10 oz. tumblers have cobalt blue handles. The set originally came with coasters. Jug, 10"h. $300-350. Tumbler, 4.75"h. $45-55 ea. *Courtesy of Catherine F. Conrady.*

Water set, possibly by Tiffin, c. 1920s. This pitcher has a blue applied handle and base. 9.27"h. $155-185. The paneled goblets have blue bases. 6"h. $45-65 ea. *Courtesy of Catherine F. Conrady.*

Footed optic stems, possibly by Cambridge, c. 1920s. This table tumbler and seltzer both have amethyst bases. Table tumbler, 4.75"h x 2.9"b. $30-40 ea. Seltzer, 2.7"h x 1.68"b. $20-30 ea. *Courtesy of Catherine F. Conrady.*

L. G. Wright water pitcher, c. 1937. According to Red Roetteis this blown pitcher with crimped top and reeded handle came from the old L. G. Wright showroom. Fenton or Beaumont probably made it as a sample for Wright. It was never produced in the Wright line. One of a kind. Value undetermined. *Courtesy of W. C. "Red" Roetteis.*

Footed custard dishes, possibly by Tiffin, c. 1920s. The bases of these paneled custards are amber. 2.75"h x 4.25"d x 2.8"b. $20-30 ea. *Courtesy of Bill McFarling.*

Wine glass, possibly by Tiffin, c. 1920-30s. This pretty wine glass has a Vaseline stem and base. The clear bowl has a panel optic design with cut decoration. 5"h x 3"d. $25-35. *Courtesy of Ben Curtis.*

Cambodia table tumbler and wines, by Utility Glass Works, Lonaconing, Maryland, c. 1920s. The bowls of these stems are shell shaped, the bases are green. Tumbler, 4.5"h x 2.5"b. Wine, 5"h x 2.3"b. $35-45 ea. *Courtesy of Catherine F. Conrady.*

Keg decanter and tumblers, possibly by McKee, c. 1920s. The decanter is 11.5"h to top of rack x 9.25"l, including spigot. Tumblers are 2.25"h x 1.75"d. $200-250. *Courtesy of Melanie Schonier.*

Water set, maker unknown, c. 1920s. These Vaseline paneled tumblers are very delicate and measure 4.25"h x 2.5"d. The basket weave pattern silver plate tray has a wooden bottom and measures 8.5"h x 7.25"l x 5.5"w. $95-125. *Courtesy of Catherine F. Conrady.*

A satin glass decanter with enamel hand painted decoration and four satin shot glasses. Maker possibly Cambridge, c. 1930s. Decanter, 7"h. Glass, 2.5"h. $100-135 set. *Courtesy of Cindy and Ben Burchfield.*

The stopper and neck of this nice Vaseline decanter are cut. Maker unknown, c. 1920s-30s. 12.5"h x 5.5"d. $125-150. *Courtesy of Catherine F. Conrady.*

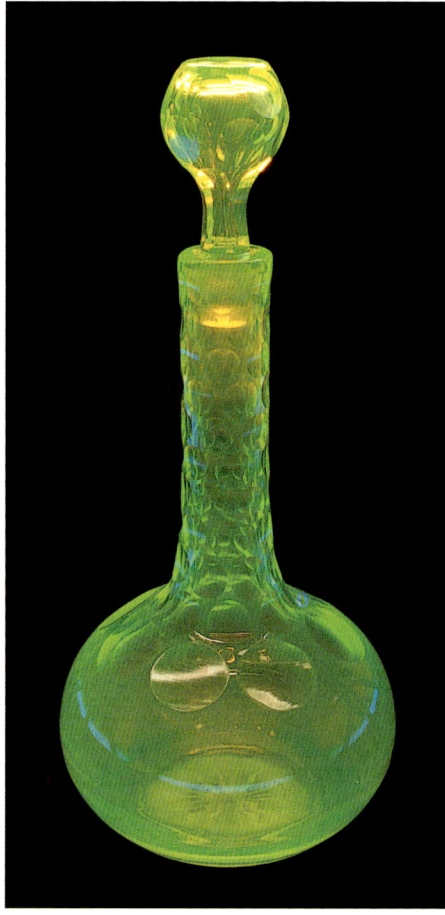

Rib Optic 11" vase by Fenton, c. 1939. $150-200. *Courtesy of Melanie Schonier.*

A footed, flared Vaseline vase, possibly by Tiffin, c. 1920s. $85-95. *Courtesy of Catherine F. Conrady.*

An opalescent *Rib Optic* lamp vase by Fenton, c. 1940s. This might have been an experimental piece. The vase is shaped like a lamp shade. 8"h. $100-125. *Courtesy of Kelvin Russell and Debra Jennings.*

The 1920s to the 1940s 61

Fenton miniatures, c. 1940s. Opalescent Vaseline pitcher, 2"h. Opalescent Vaseline vase, 1.85"h. $65-75 ea. *Courtesy of Kelvin Russell and Debra Jennings.*

"Shari" dresser set by McKee, c. 1930s. Two views are shown for detail. The name "Shari" is marked in the base mold on both sides. The base has four slots to hold Shari compacts and perfumes. The cover has a floral design with birds and butterflies. 4"h x 7"l x 2.2"w. $175-200. *Courtesy of Melanie Schonier.*

Dot Optic perfumizer made by Fenton for De Vilbiss, c. 1940s. 4.25"h x 3.25"d. $95-125. *Courtesy of Cindy and Ben Burchfield.*

Puff box by Fostoria, c. 1920s. 1"h x 4"d. $65-85. *Courtesy of Sharron and Jay Reynolds.*

Perfume #585 by Cambridge Glass Co., c. 1920-30s. This frosted topaz perfume has a beehive stopper and enamel decoration. The flowers are mustard colored with orange stripes and black dots under natural light. 4.25"h x 1.7"d x 1.85"b. $65-85. *Courtesy of Catherine F. Conrady.*

Perfumizers, possibly by Tiffin, c. 1920-30s. 7"h. $100-125 ea. *Courtesy of Catherine F. Conrady.*

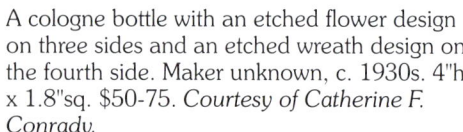

A cologne bottle with an etched flower design on three sides and an etched wreath design on the fourth side. Maker unknown, c. 1930s. 4"h x 1.8"sq. $50-75. *Courtesy of Catherine F. Conrady.*

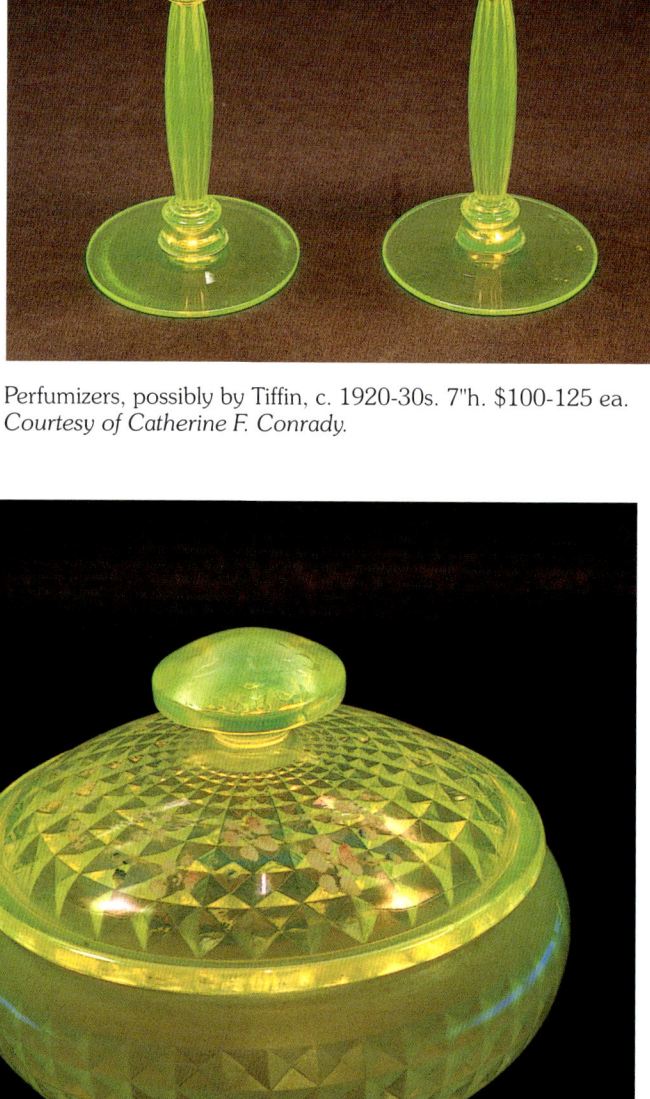

Diamond Optic iridescent stretch puff box by Fenton, c. 1920-30s. 3.75"h x 4.5"d. $75-95. *Courtesy of Cindy and Ben Burchfield.*

The 1920s to the 1940s   63

Cut plate, maker possibly Fostoria, c. 1920-30s. 7.5"d. $30-40. *Courtesy of Catherine F. Conrady.*

Beaded Block plate made by Imperial Glass Company, c. 1927-1930s. Be very careful when purchasing this plate. This collector had two that were exactly the same color. One glowed under black light the other did not. 8"sq. $20-30. *Courtesy of Catherine F. Conrady.*

Candy jar with cut flower and leaf design by Fostoria, c. 1924-27. 6.25"h x 4.8"d. $75-95. *Courtesy of Melanie Schonier.*

The 1920s to the 1940s

A footed, fan shaped nappy with opalescent rim and handle, possibly Duncan & Miller, c. 1940s. 3.25"h x 6"l x 5.75"w. $50-60.

A #16258 satin glass 9" wall vase by Tiffin, c. 1920-30s. $75-120. *Courtesy of Catherine F. Conrady.*

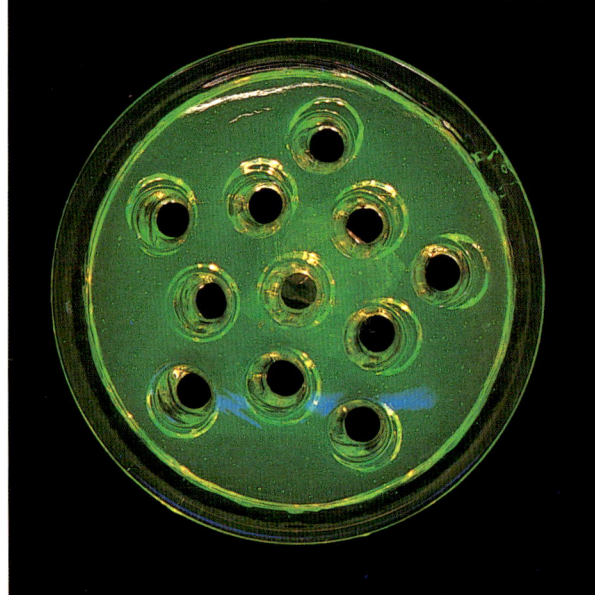

A 1920s flower frog. 0.92"h x 3"d. $8-12. *Courtesy of Catherine F. Conrady.*

Automobile flower vases that were popular in the late 1920s. These vases were added to the interior door post of a car and held live flowers. An ad from a 1926 publication furnished by Frank and Melissa Keathley attributes a similar vase that is shown on pg. 77 of my first volume, *The Picture Book of Vaseline Glass*, to Moswell. Left vase, 6.25"l. Right vase, 7.25"l. $75-125 ea. *Courtesy of Catherine F. Conrady.*

A decorative Vaseline Glass thermometer. Maker unknown, c. 1930s. 5.75"h x 1.5"sq.b. $50-75. Courtesy of Catherine F. Conrady.

Daisy & Button hand vase by Fenton, c. 1937-39. 6.1"h. $45-55. Courtesy of Catherine F. Conrady.

Corn Vase by L. G. Wright, c. 1939. Dugan Glass Co. originally made the corn vase about 1905. Wright bought the mold in 1939 and produced Vaseline opalescent at that time. This reproduction has a smooth top, the original has a scalloped top (see *The Picture Book of Vaseline Glass*, pg. 44-45). The space between the ear and shuck that attaches to the base is solid in the reproduction. 7.25"h. $75-85. Courtesy of Catherine F. Conrady.

Vaseline drawer pulls, maker unknown, c. 1920-30s. 2"d. $50-70 pr.

#76 canary satin glass candleholders by Tiffin, c. 1920s. 9"h x 4.25"b. $95-125 pr. *Courtesy of Catherine F. Conrady.*

Cambridge candlesticks #1595, c. 1920s. These candlesticks have hollow bases and five rings around the columns. 8.5"h x 4"b. $100-110 pr. *Courtesy of Catherine F. Conrady.*

A pair of topaz six sided iridescent stretch glass candlesticks, possibly H. Northwood & Co. #658, c. 1916-25. $125-150 pr. *Courtesy of Catherine F. Conrady.*

The 1920s to the 1940s 67

Two candlesticks. The four sided satin glass candlestick on the left is by Westmoreland, c. 1920s. 7"h x 3.25"sq.b. $40-50. The long column, hexagonal base topaz iridescent candlestick on the right is Fenton's No. 449, c. 1920s. 8.5"h x 3.75"b. $120-130. *Courtesy of Catherine F. Conrady.*

No. 315 canary iridescent stretch glass candleholders by Tiffin, c. 1920s. 9.75"h x 4.6"b. $125-150 pr. *Courtesy of Catherine F. Conrady.*

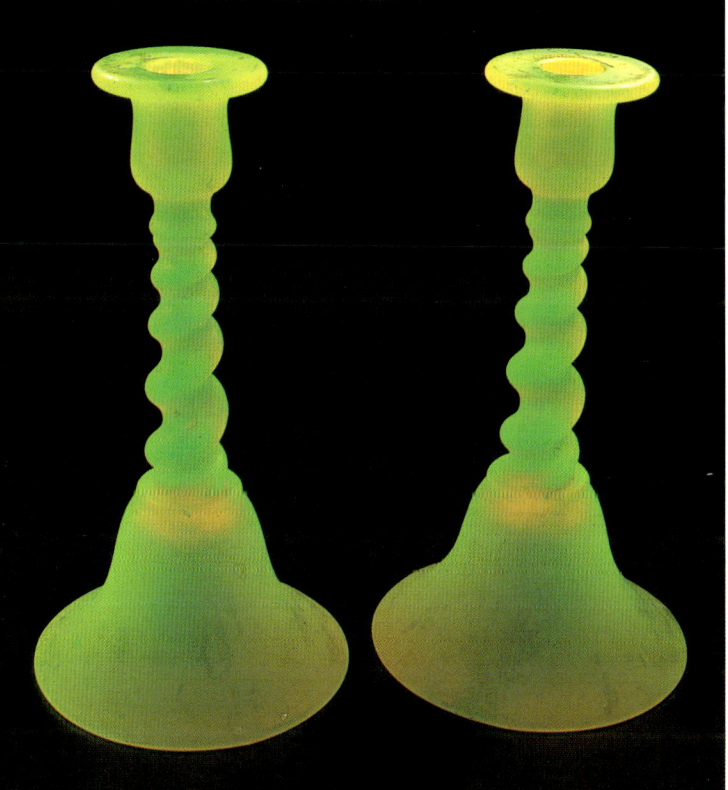

No. 315 canary satin glass candleholders by Tiffin, c. 1920s. 9.75"h x 5"b. $100-125 pr. *Courtesy of Catherine F. Conrady.*

Candlesticks. On the left a hollow base Vaseline candleholder, possibly Tiffin's #79, c. 1920s. 6.3"h x 4.25"b. $55-75. On the right a #2269 single light Vaseline candlestick with white trim by Fostoria, c. 1920s. 6"h x 3.8"b. $65-70. *Courtesy of Catherine F. Conrady.*

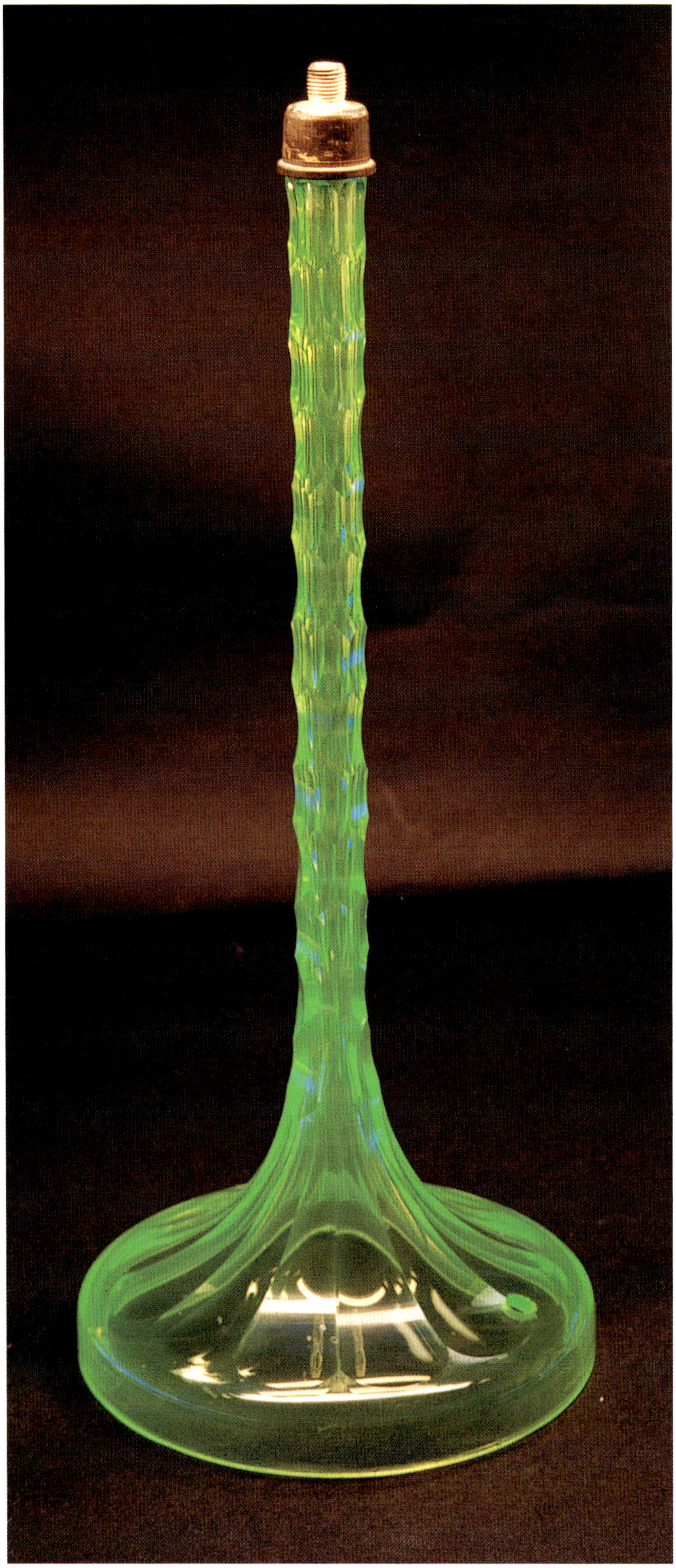

Stick lamps by Westmoreland, c. 1920s. This honeycomb pattern vanity lamp is pictured with and without a shade. 14.24"h x 6"b; 21.25"h x 6"b. $75-95. *Courtesy of Catherine F. Conrady and Cindy and Ben Burchfield.*

The 1920s to the 1940s 69

A McKee Tambour art glass clock, c. 1920-30s. 6"h x 14"l x 4"w. $575-625. *Courtesy of Betty and Del Kerr.*

Hobnail opalescent squat jug and tumblers, probably by Fenton, c. 1940s. Jug, 5"h x 5.25"d. $75-95. Tumbler, 3.4"h x 2.5"d. $15-25. *Courtesy of Catherine F. Conrady.*

Radium Emanator Filter Co. water bottle by McKee Glass Co., c. 1920s. 21"h x 9"d. $1200-1250. *Courtesy of Melanie Schonier.*

Chapter IV
The 1950s to the Present

Cactus single horn epergne by Fenton, c. 1959. 7.5"h x 9.5"w. $450-500. *Courtesy of Cindy and Ben Burchfield.*

Cactus basket by Fenton, c. 1959. 10.5"h x 10"l x 7.5"w. $300-350. *Courtesy of Melanie Schonier.*

The 1950s to the Present 71

An *Heirloom* pate by Fostoria, c. 1959-1970. 17"d. $100-125. *Courtesy of Melanie Schonier.*

Heirloom bowl. 3.7"h x 12.75"l x 5.5"w. $75-100. *Courtesy of Keri Davis.*

Heirloom charm set. $250-300. *Courtesy of Melanie Schonier.*

Heirloom epergne. 8.5"h x 13"l x 8"w. $155-165. *Courtesy of Melanie Schonier.*

Thumbprint candy box by Fenton. Thought to have been made as samples sometime in the early 1960s. The bowl has opalescence around the top. $100-125. *Courtesy of Janet Wilke.*

Thumbprint basket by Fenton, c. 1960s. 9"h x 8.25"d. $175-195. *Courtesy of Catherine F. Conrady.*

Daisy and Fern (Fern) wedding bowl by L. G. Wright Glass Co., c. 1979. Wright purchased the molds for this pattern in the late 1930s and Fenton produced the pattern exclusively for Wright for many years. In the 1990s, Fenton included the pattern in their regular line but changed the daisy slightly. The Wright daisy has straight petals like this example. The petals of the Fenton daisy appear to be blowing in the wind. 4"h x 10.5"d. $85-95. *Courtesy of Catherine F. Conrady.*

The 1950s to the Present

Daisy and Fern insert for pickle jar by L. G. Wright Glass Co., c. mid 1960s. 5"h x 3.25"d. $50-75. *Courtesy of Lena Lou Staton.*

A fluted *Daisy and Fern* satin finish barber bottle with a rolled lip and ground pontil by L. G. Wright Glass Co., c. 1960s. 7.25"h x 3.75"d. $125-150. *Courtesy of Lena Lou Staton.*

Daisy and Fern cruet by L. G. Wright Glass Co., c. 1960s. 6.5"h x 3.45"d. $100-125. *Courtesy of Catherine F. Conrady.*

Opalescent Dot tumbler by L. G. Wright Glass Co., c. 1960s, 3.75"h x 2.9"d. $45-50. *Courtesy of Lena Lou Staton.*

The 1950s to the Present 75

Daisy & Button spooner and pitcher. The spooner on the left is marked with L. G. Wright logo W with underline in a circle, c. 1974. 4.5"h x 3.3"d. $40-60. The maker and circa date of the pitcher are unknown. 6.75"h x 3.75"d. $75-95. *Courtesy of Catherine F. Conrady.*

Opal Open ivy bowl made by Fenton for L. G Wright, c. 1960s. This is a reproduction of the Northwood pattern of 1910. The loops on the base are solid. 7.5"h x 5.7"d x 4"b. $65-85. *Courtesy of Catherine F. Conrady.*

Frosted Stork bread plate imported in Vaseline from Korea or Taiwan and sold by A. A. Importing Co. Inc., c. 1975. This pattern was originally produced in all clear and clear-and-frosted by Crystal Glass Co. of Ohio, c. 1880. 11.75"l x 8"w. $50-75. *Courtesy of Catherine F. Conrady.*

The 1950s to the Present

Wildflower footed sauces by L. G. Wright Glass Co., c. 1968. 2.35"h x 4"d. $20-30. *Courtesy of Catherine F. Conrady.*

A pressed satin glass boat bowl with an imitation cut glass pattern. Maker unknown, c. possibly 1950s-60s. 4.5"h x 11"l x 7.75"w. $45-65. *Courtesy of Cindy and Ben Burchfield.*

Stork spooner reproduced in Korea or Taiwan and sold by A. A. Importing Co. Inc., c. 1982. This spooner has three different views of the stork (crane). In the oval pictured the crane is standing straight, in another oval the crane is dipping into the water, in the third oval the crane has a fish in its mouth. 5.3"h x 3.9"d. $20-40. *Courtesy of Catherine F. Conrady.*

Wildflower goblet by L. G. Wright Glass Co., c. 1968. This pattern was originally produced by Adams & Company, c. 1874 and reissued from Factory A (Adams) of U. S. Glass Co. after 1891. The detail of the pattern is not as distinct in the reproduction. 5.95"h x 3.25"d. $38-40. *Courtesy of Catherine F. Conrady.*

A primitive looking Vaseline and blue plate. Maker unknown, c. possibly 1950s. 8"d. $15-20. *Courtesy of Catherine F. Conrady.*

The 1950s to the Present 77

A *Hobnail* opalescent dish. Maker and circa date unknown. The handles are solid with hobnails on them. Help with identification would be appreciated. 2"h x 7"l x 5.4"w. $35-45. *Courtesy of Catherine F. Conrady.*

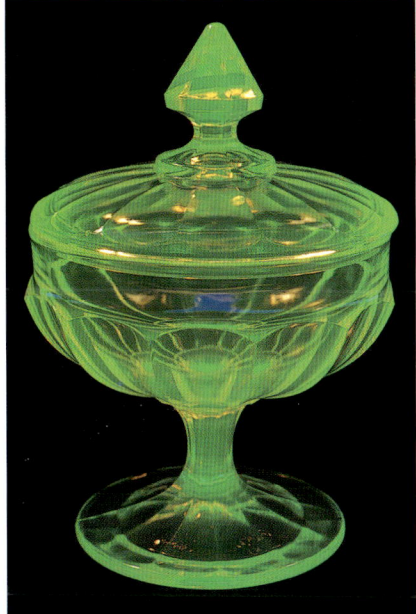

A footed candy dish. Maker and circa date unknown. Help with identification would be appreciated. 6.25"h x 4.25"d x 3.35"b. $45-55. *Courtesy of Catherine F. Conrady.*

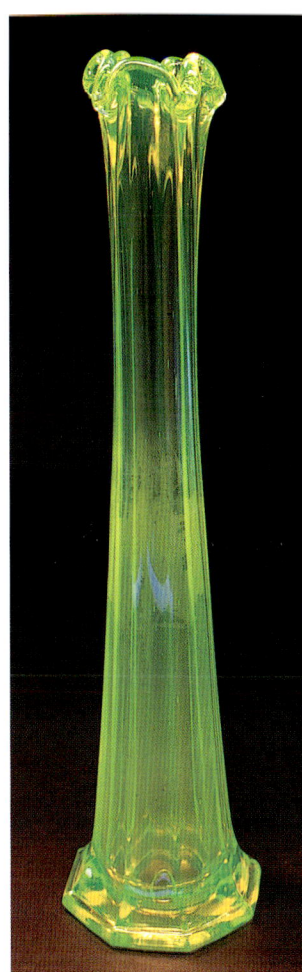

A tall, slender ribbed Vaseline vase with crimped top. Possibly Westmoreland, c. 1950-1980. 11.5"h. $20-30. *Courtesy of Catherine F. Conrady.*

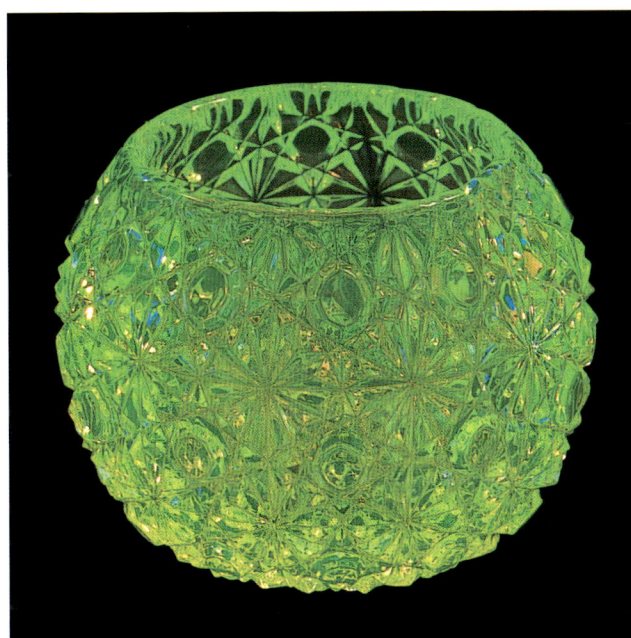

A *Daisy & Button* rose bowl. Maker and circa date unknown. The pattern is very sharp and well defined. Help with identification would be appreciated. 2.7"h x 3.6"d. $40-50. *Courtesy of Catherine F. Conrady.*

Daisy & Button Star sauce dishes by L. G. Wright Glass Co., c. 1950-60s. Compare this piece to the Hobbs Star bowl in Chapter II (see p. 26) and notice the difference in the smooth grooves. They meet in the Hobbs piece and do not in the Wright piece. 1.25"h x 5.5"d. $20-25 ea. *Courtesy of Catherine F. Conrady.*

Satin glass covered hen by L. G. Wright Glass Co., c. late 1940s-1960s. This hen has opalescence on the head and tail. 3.75"h x 7.5"l x 5.5"w. $115-125. *Courtesy of Catherine F. Conrady.*

Portrait plate *"First Lady of Glass Elizabeth Degenhart,"* c. 1970s. This plate bears the Degenhart logo, a D in a heart. 5.6"d. $65-75. *Courtesy of Catherine F. Conrady.*

An Irish Waterford fairy lite by Westmoreland Glass, c. 1960s-70s. This satin glass fairy lamp with hand painted orange flowers and a Westmoreland sticker that appears to be original is 6.5"h x 4.5"d. $65-75. *Courtesy of Catherine F. Conrady.*

Robin on Nest by Degenhart, c. 1976. 4.5"h x 5.5"l x 4.25"w. $50-60. Boyd is currently producing this mold. The Boyd pieces are marked. $25-35. *Courtesy of Catherine F. Conrady.*

A Fenton drapery pattern Vaseline opalescent vase, c. 2000. 4.5"h. $55-60.

The 1950s to the Present   79

Boyd paperweight. The paperweight is shaped like the Boyd logo, a diamond with a B in the center, and has "Boyd Crystal Art Glass" around the edges. 3"l x 2.5"w. $35-40. *Courtesy of Catherine F. Conrady.*

Cullet weighing three pounds. Cullet by definition is scraps of waste glass that can be melted to make new pieces of glass. 3.75"h x 6.5"l x 3"w. *Courtesy of Catherine F. Conrady.*

Cactus salt and pepper by Summit Art Glass, c. late 1990s. 3.37"h x 1.75"d. $25-30. *Courtesy of Catherine F. Conrady.*

Daisy & Button toothpick with opalescent top by L. G. Wright, c. 1960s. 3.9"h x 3.3"l x 2"w. $25-35. *Courtesy of Catherine F. Conrady.*

Measuring cup with reamer by Summit Art Glass, c. 1980s; Rosso Glass Co., c. 2000-01. 5.25"h x 3.3"d. $35-40. *Courtesy of Catherine F. Conrady.*

The 1950s to the Present

A Honey Jar with hand painted bees by Boyd's Crystal Art Glass, c. 1999. 5"h x 3.75"b. $30-40. *Courtesy of Catherine F. Conrady.*

Hand pin tray. The Degenhart logo can be seen in the palm of this hand. c. 1970s. Boyd has reissued this piece marked with the Boyd logo. 1.6"h x 5"l x 2.1"w. $20-25. *Courtesy of Catherine F. Conrady.*

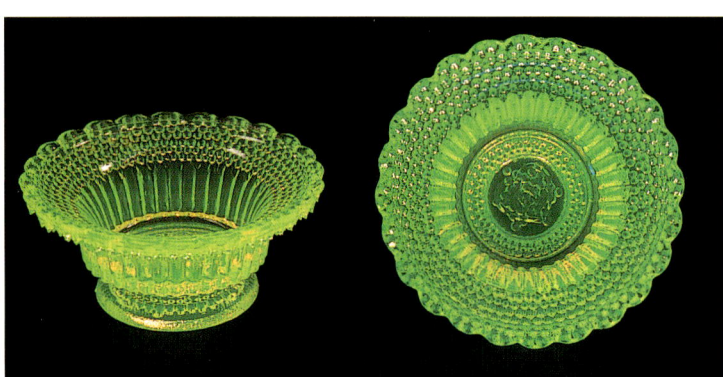

Degenhart salts signed with the Degenhart logo, a D inside a heart, c. 1970s. 1.5"h x 3.25"d. $25-35 ea. *Courtesy of Catherine F. Conrady.*

Skate toothpick by Boyd's Crystal Art Glass, c. 1993-98. All Boyd glass is marked with the Diamond B logo. 4.25"h x 2.89"l x 1.1"w. $15-20. *Courtesy of Catherine F. Conrady.*

Tomahawk by Degenhart, c. 1970s. This tomahawk has recently been produced by Boyd and will be marked with the Boyd logo. 7.3"l. $35-45. *Courtesy of Catherine F. Conrady.*

The 1950s to the Present

Bottoms Up Cup by Summit Art Glass, c. mid 1980s and again 1990-2000. 3"h x 2.5"b. $18-20. *Courtesy of Catherine F. Conrady.*

A piano novelty by Summit Art Glass, c. 1990s. This was originally a candy dish. 2.75"h x 3"w. $18-25. *Courtesy of Catherine F. Conrady.*

Pickle dish by Boyd's Crystal Art Glass, c. 1993-98. This dish has the Boyd logo. In the bottom is a picture of a woman and the inscription "Loves Request Is Pickles." 1.6"h x 9.25"l x 5.1"w. $25-35. *Courtesy of Catherine F. Conrady.*

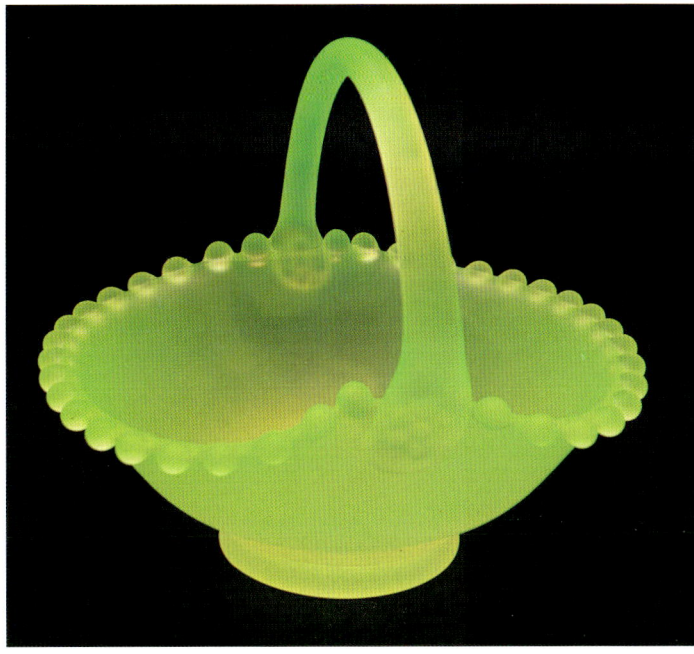

Candlewick satin 5" basket made for Rosso Glass, c. 2000. Only 230 of these baskets were available. $55-65.

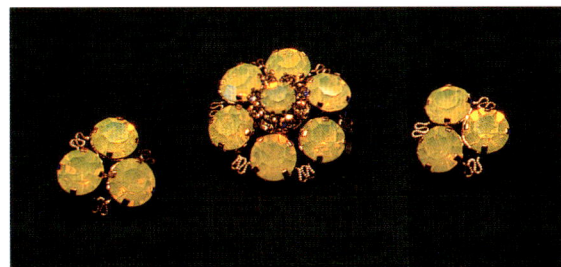

A Vaseline brooch and earring set. The faceted Vaseline stones are prong-set. Maker unknown, c. possibly 1950-60s. Brooch, 1.5"d. Earring, 0.75"d. $75-100 set. *Courtesy of Sharron and Jay Reynolds.*

A lovely pin with a prong-set, emerald cut Vaseline stone and silver tone mounting, c. possibly 1960s. 4"l x 3"w. $65-85. *Courtesy of Marlene J. King.*

82 The 1950s to the Present

A pin with silver tone mounting and Vaseline teardrops. Maker unknown, c. possibly 1960s. Mounting, 3.5"l x 2.37"w. Vaseline drops, 0.75"l. $65-85. *Courtesy of Sharyn Ferre.*

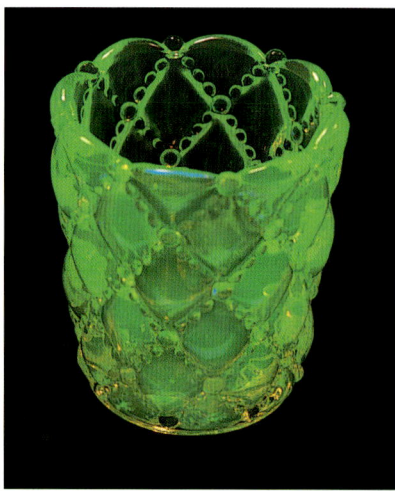

Quilted Bead votive by Brooke Glass, c. 1980-1990s. This pattern is sometimes called *Beaded Diamond*. 2.5"h. $10-15. *Courtesy of Lena Lou Staton.*

A frosted opalescent figural snail by Fenton, c. 1990s. 2.75"h x 4.5"l x 2"w. $35-45. *Courtesy of Lena Lou Staton.*

An 18" necklace made with Vaseline Czech beads by Bruce P. Schiwitz, c. 2000. $45-55. *Courtesy of Ben Curtis.*

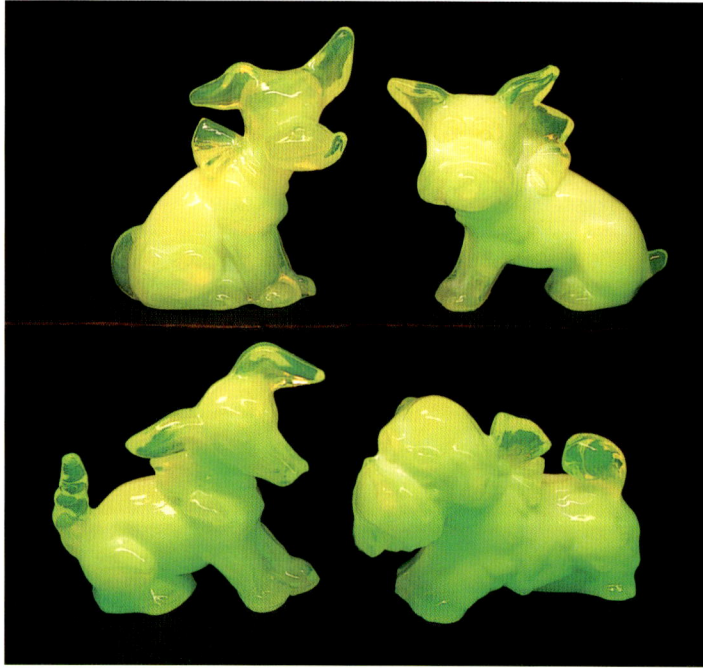

Parlor Pups by Boyd's Crystal Art Glass, c. 1993-98. Back row, left to right: Parlor Pup #3, 3.62"h; Parlor Pup #1, 3.13"h. Front row, left to right: Parlor Pup #4, 3.43"h; Parlor Pup #2, 2.9"h. $45-50 set. *Courtesy of Ben Curtis.*

The 1950s to the Present 83

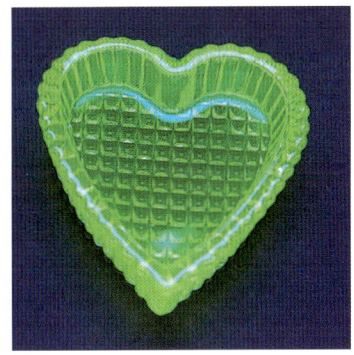

One inch heart salt by Summit, c. 1998-2000. $8-12. *Courtesy of Linda Wilder.*

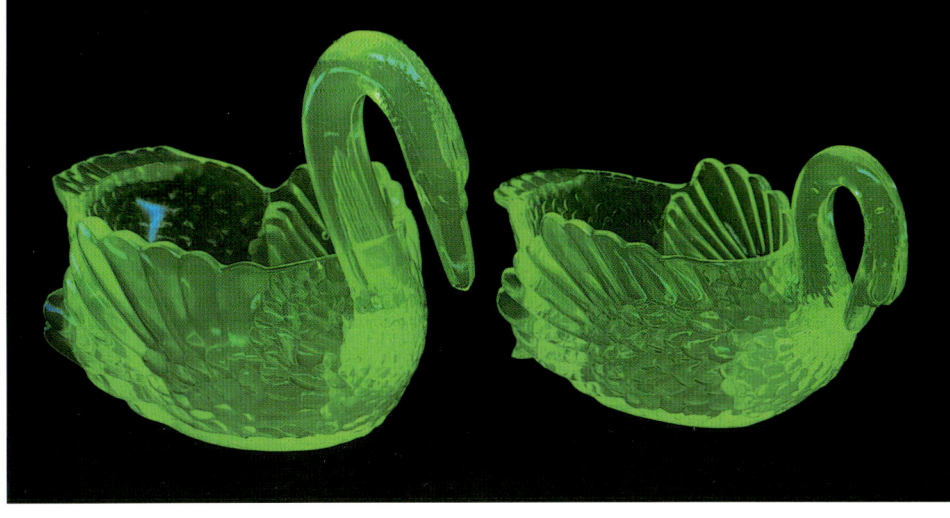

Swans by Summit Art Glass, c. 2001. These swans are from original Cambridge molds and have never before been made in Vaseline. Variation in neck positions and the presence of bubbles are common. 6.5" swan. $35-40. 8.5" swan. $50-60. *Courtesy of Bruce P. Schiwitz.*

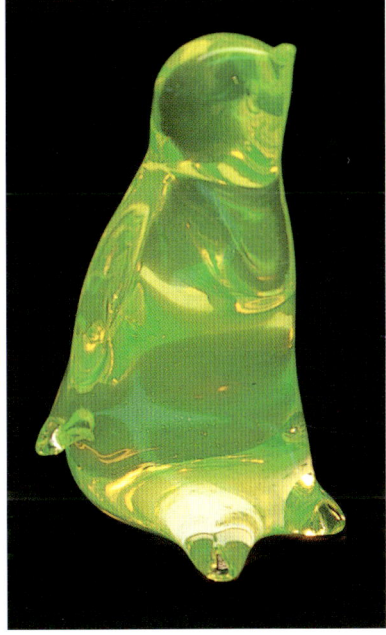

Penguin by Gibson Glass, c. 2001. $22-26. *Courtesy of Bruce P. Schiwitz.*

A satin swan from The National Heisey Museum gift shop. Mosser Glass, c. 1998, made it for the Heisey Collectors of America, Inc. It is marked on the right side of the tail "HCA 98 M." 7.5"l x 4.25"d. $25-35. *Courtesy of Linda Wilder.*

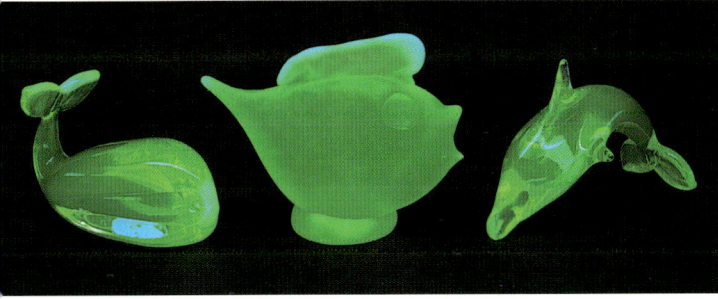

Gibson Glass grouping, c. 2001. Whale with opalescence on nose and tail, 4"l. $22-25. Satin fish with opalescence on top, 3.4"h x 4.35"l. $30-35. Dolphin, 4.15"l. $28-32. *Courtesy of Bruce P. Schiwitz.*

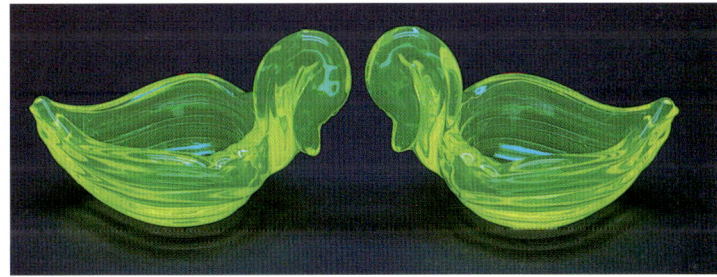

Swans by Mosser Glass, c. 1998. Description same as for satin swan above. 3"l x 1.9"w. $8-12. *Courtesy of Linda Wilder.*

84   The 1950s to the Present

Vaseline hammer, custom made. This is the official gavel of the VGCI and is passed from president to president. The 12"l hammer has a hollow handle. The head is 4.75"l x 2"d and has bubble inclusions. $50-75. *Courtesy of Madolyn R. Courter.*

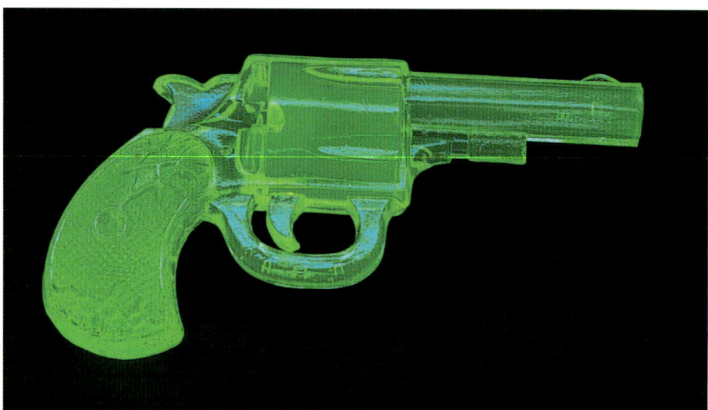

Hand Gun by Summit Art Glass, c. 2001. Made from a Westmoreland mold. 5"l. $22-27. *Courtesy of Bruce P. Schiwitz.*

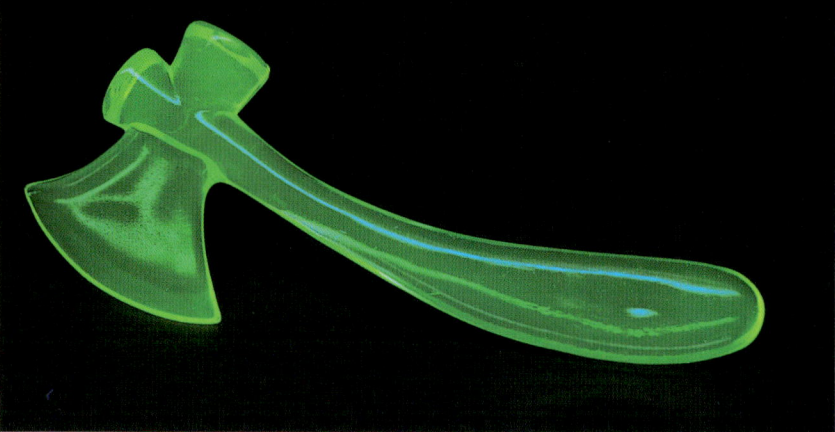

Hatchet by Summit Art Glass, c. 2001. Made from a Westmoreland mold. 5.75"l. $22-27. *Courtesy of Bruce P. Schiwitz.*

Queen's cake stand by Mosser Glass, c. 1998-2000. Mosser is also reproducing other pieces of this pattern (butter dish, water set, compote). 5"h x 9.5"d. $55-65. *Courtesy of Linda Wilder.*

The 1950s to the Present 85

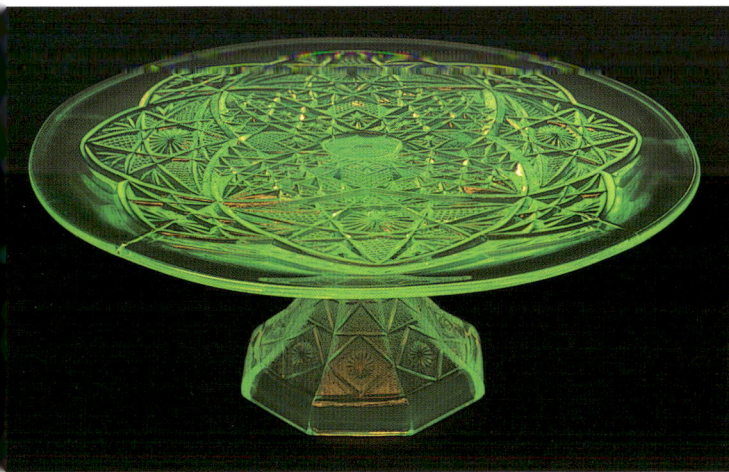

Cake stand by Mosser Glass, c. late 1990s. 5"h x 12.25"d. $55-75. *Courtesy of Linda Wilder.*

A spittoon made by Gibson Glass exclusively for Vaseline Glass Collectors, Inc., c. 2001. Gibson dates most of its glass on the bottom. 4"h x 4.25"d. $35.

Cherry Thumbprint butter dish by Mosser Glass, c. 2001. This piece bears the Mosser M. This pattern is also known as *Cherry* or *Cherry Cable*. One will also see the water set in this line by Mosser and in the future there are plans for the bowl, spooner, goblet, and cracker jar all in Vaseline. 5.75"h x 7.75"d. $35-45. *Courtesy of Bruce P. Schiwitz.*

Oil lamps by Mosser Glass, c. 2001. These measure 14.5" and bear the Mosser logo, an M inside the state of Ohio. Paneled lamp, $90-95. *Courtesy of Bruce P. Schiwitz.* Daisy and Fern lamp, $100-110. *Courtesy of W. C. "Red" Roetteis.*

The 1950s to the Present

Star ashtray by Summit Art Glass, c. 2001. This ashtray is made from a Cambridge mold and is 5"d. $14-17. *Courtesy of Bruce P. Schiwitz.*

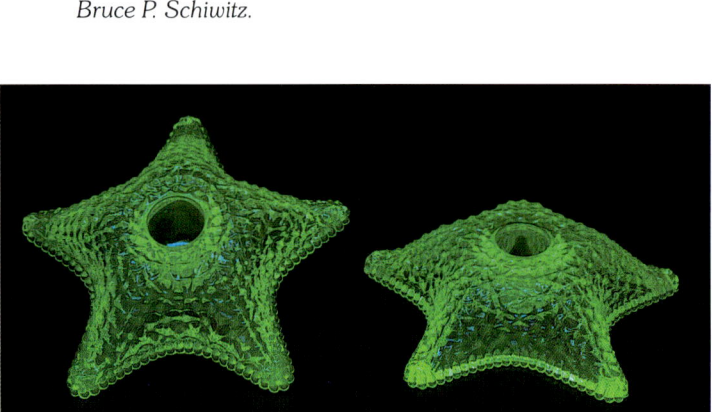

Starfish candleholders by Summit Art Glass, c. 2000. Summit made these exclusively for Irene Tebo of Vaseline Glass Palace. $45 pr. *Courtesy of Bruce P. Schiwitz.*

Covered boxes by Summit Art Glass, c. 2001. The *Mount Vernon* covered box measures 2.5"h x 6"l x 4.5"w. $28-32. The *Turtle* candy dish measures 2.25"h x 7.5"l x 4.25"w. This piece, made from a Westmoreland mold, was originally a cigarette box. $28-32. *Courtesy of Bruce P. Schiwitz.*

A bird egg cup by Summit Art Glass, marked with the logo V inside a circle, c. 2001. 2.4"h x 2.2"d. $15-20. A bird vase or footed spooner made for Rosso Glass, c. 2001. 5.75"h x 4.5"d. $35-45. *Courtesy of Bruce P. Schiwitz.*

Acorn spooner by Mosser Glass, c. 2001. Notice that the space between the stem and the base is open, which would lead one to believe that the piece is old. It is not. 5"h x 3.9"d. $35-40. *Courtesy of Bruce P. Schiwitz.*

The 1950s to the Present   87

A Bonsai style tree made by Tracy K. Salava using 20 gauge wire with uranium glass beads for leaves and the pebbles in the holder. One of a kind. 8"h. *Courtesy of Tracy K. Salava.*

A mini apple paperweight by Gibson Glass, c. 1998. This attractive little paperweight has an opalescent reverse swirl pattern and measures 2.6"h x 1.8"d. $20-25. *Courtesy of Linda Wilder.*

Gibson Glass grouping, c. 2001. Blown egg iridized novelty on left, 2.47"l x 1.85"d. $22-28. *Hanging Heart* paperweight in the center. The hearts are dark blue. 3"h x 2.35"d. $75-80. Blown egg white spatter novelty on right, 2.47"l x 1.85"d. $22-28. *Courtesy of Bruce P. Schiwitz.*

Long Stem Flowers by Gibson Glass, c. 2001. This type flower can be found in lengths from 6" to 10" with varying degrees of opalescence and in varying shapes. Shown are the 10", 9", and 8" lengths. $20-30 ea. *Courtesy of Bruce P. Schiwitz.*

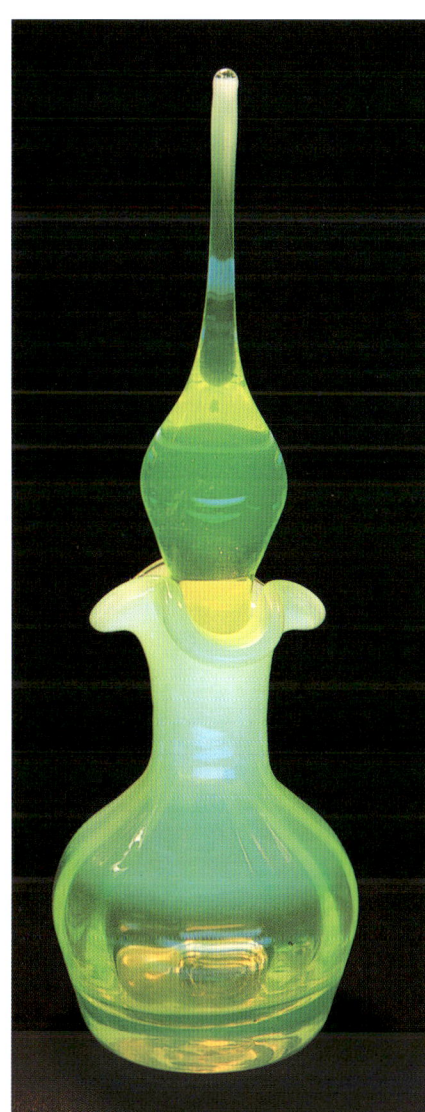

A Vaseline opalescent perfume bottle made by Gibson Glass in 2000 exclusively for the Vaseline Glass Collectors, Inc. 6.75"h x 2.45"d. $50-60.

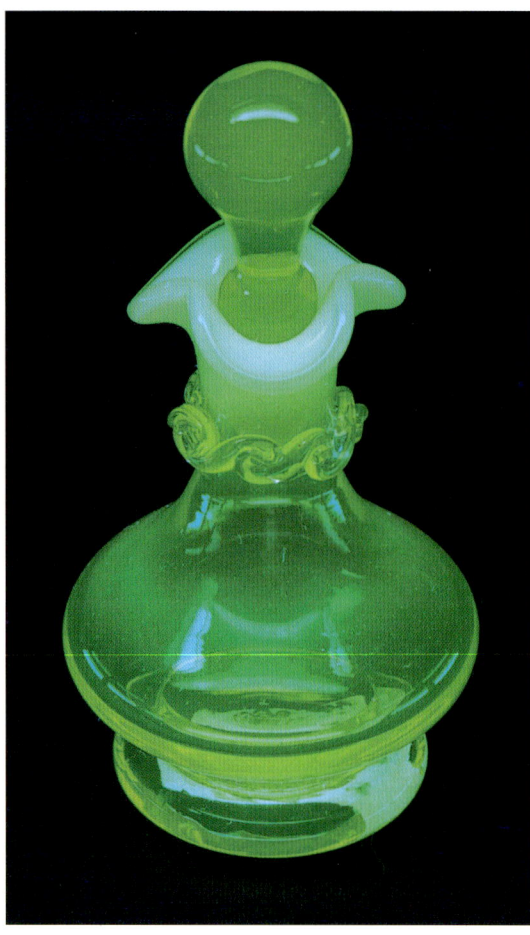

A perfume by Gibson Glass, c. 1999. 5"h x 2.7"d. $50-60. *Courtesy of Bruce P. Schiwitz.*

A signed grouping by Ron Lukian, c. 2000. Left to right: Perfume 3.5"h x 2.1"d. $55-65. *Courtesy of Bruce P. Schiwitz.* Perfume 4.6"h x 2.75"d. $75-85. *Courtesy of Sharron and Jay Reynolds.* Perfume, 4.4"h x 2.1"d. $70-80. *Courtesy of Bruce P. Schiwitz.* Ring holder, 4.5"h x 1.7"b. $25-35. *Courtesy of Sharron and Jay Reynolds.*

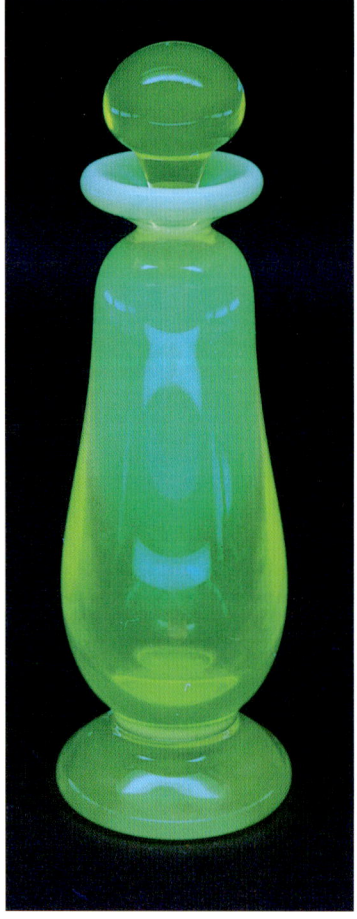

A signed perfume by Ron Lukian, c. 2000. 4.9"h x 1.45"d. $50-70. *Courtesy of Bruce P. Schiwitz.*

Sea Serpent perfume by Ed Pennebaker, c. 1999. 3.65"h without dauber x 2.9"w. $25-45. *Courtesy of Sharron and Jay Reynolds.*

The 1950s to the Present   89

This unusual piece is one of a kind made by James Whitehurst for the owner after he delivered a purchase late. The bottom is signed and inscribed with the owner's e-mail name and "late," c. 2001. 4.75"h. *Courtesy of Sharron and Jay Reynolds.*

Spiral Optic fairy light by Fenton, c. 2001. This one piece fairy light was made exclusively for Fenton Art Glass Collectors of America Inc. On the bottom there is a butterfly in an oval with FAGCA 2001 around it. 5.25"h x 7.1"d. $85-100. *Courtesy of Janet Wilke.*

Vases by Gibson Glass, c. 2001. These vases are signed on the bottom like most Gibson glass. Opalescent stripe vase, 6"h x 4.2"d. Opalescent rib vase, 6.5"h x 4.2"d. $70-75 ea. *Courtesy of Bruce P. Schiwitz.*

Hanging Heart vase by Gibson Glass, c. 2001. The standard color is amethyst in the *Hanging Heart* pattern, however bright blue and dark blue do exist. All Gibson glass is handmade, therefore measurements can vary by 10%. 6.5"h x 4.1"d. $110-120. *Courtesy of Bruce P. Schiwitz.*

Hanging Heart vases by Gibson Glass, c. 2001. Flared top vase, 6.25"h x 3.9"d. $95-100. Ruffle top vase, 6.5"h x 3.45"d. $75-85. *Courtesy of Bruce P. Schiwitz.*

Jack-in-the-Pulpit vases by Gibson Glass, c. 2001. Coin Dot vase, 7.1"h x 3.15"b. $65-70. Crackle vase, 8"h x 3.4"d. $45-50. *Courtesy of Bruce P. Schiwitz.*

The 1950s to the Present 91

Bud vase by Gibson Glass, c. 2001. 6.25"h x 2.1"b. $30-35. *Courtesy of Bruce P. Schiwitz.*

Water set by Gibson Glass, c. 1997. Red Roetteis, long time employee of L. G. Wright and author of *The L. G. Wright Glass Company*, provided the following information about this water set. Northwood or Duncan originally owned the mold for this pattern, Harvest Flower. L. G. Wright purchased the mold. Gibson then borrowed the mold from Wright and produced this water set in 1997. Gibson no longer has the mold. It sold at the L. G. Wright auction. Pitcher, 11"h x 5.5"b. Tumbler, 4.75"h x 2.9"d. $380-420 set. *Courtesy of W. C. "Red" Roetteis.*

Diamond Lace epergne by Fenton, c. 2001. This iridized epergne has black trim that looks a little silver due to the iridescence. The Fenton number is 4808 T8. 10"h. $225-235. *Courtesy of Bruce P. Schiwitz.*

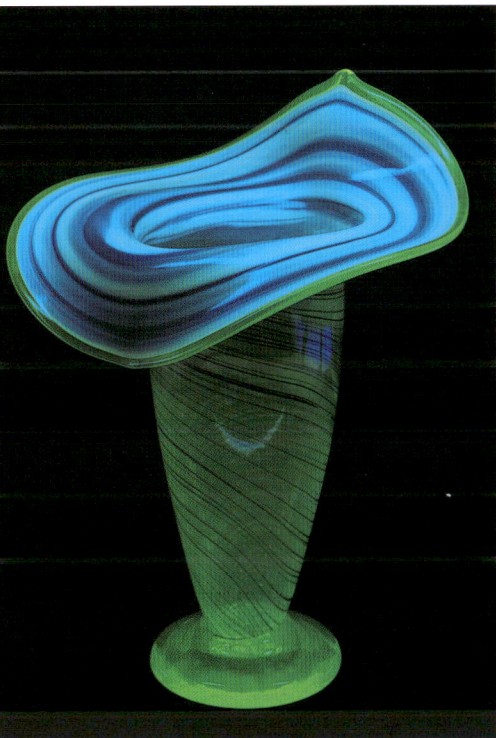

Jack-in-the-Pulpit vase by James Whitehurst, c. 2001. This large blown vase has an opalescent top with purple and blue swirl threading around the body. 11.5"h x 8.75"d top. $125-150. *Courtesy of Sharron and Jay Reynolds.*

Elite vase #6564 by Fenton, c. 2001. This iridized vase measures 8.25"h x 3.4"b. $40-42. *Courtesy of Bruce P. Schiwitz.*

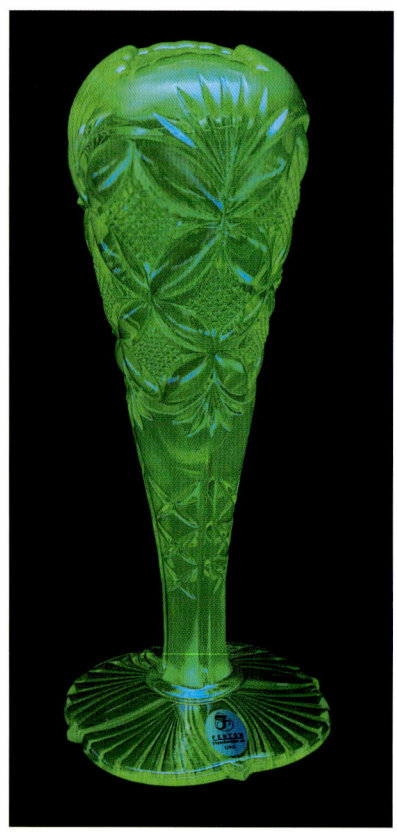

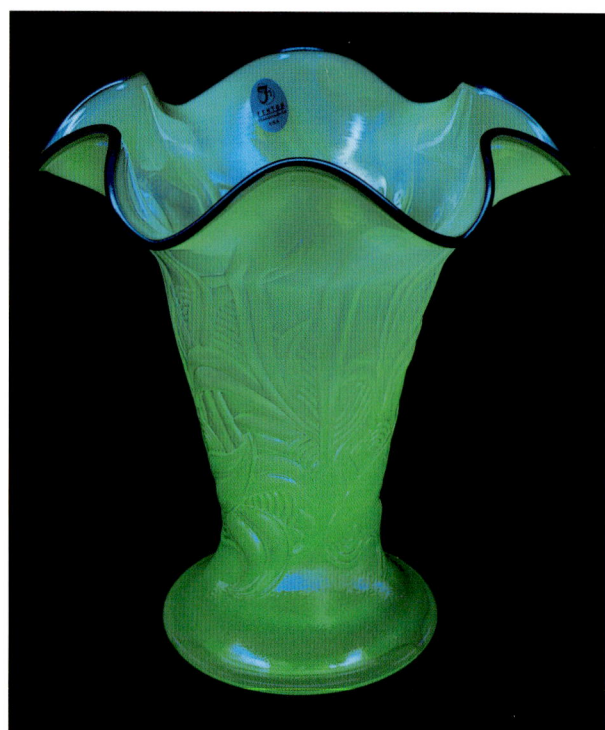

Fenton vase #6852, c. 2001. This iridized vase measures 7"h x 3.7"b. $85-89. *Courtesy of Bruce P. Schiwitz.*

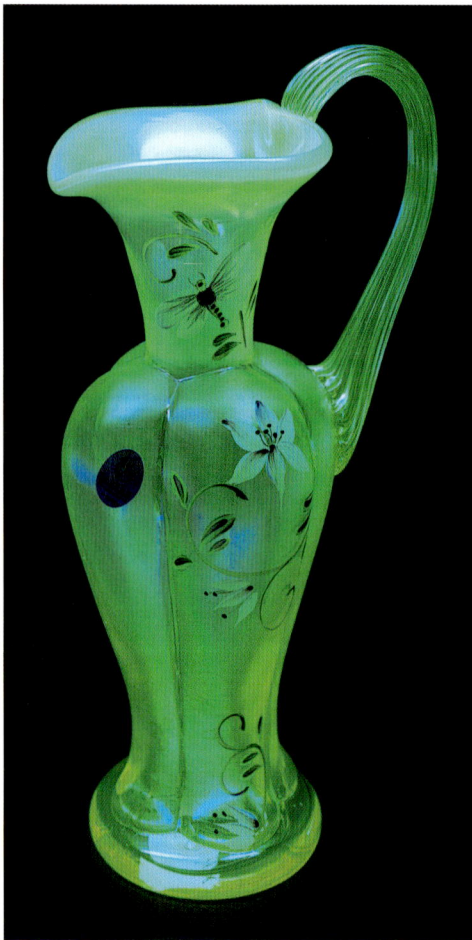

Lily Trails ewer #6365 by Fenton, c. 2001. This is an iridized, hand painted, family signature piece. 9"h. $130-136. *Courtesy of Bruce P. Schiwitz.*

Fenton "Meadow Poppies" vase from the Connoisseur Collection, c. 2001. The card with this beautiful piece states "Handcrafted from 1981 Fenton mold. The glistening Topaz Amberina shade is achieved by carefully blowing a gold Ruby roll with a layer of Topaz glass. Frances Burton designer." Limited edition 175/1750. 9.5"h. $225-245. *Courtesy of Janet Wilke.*

Chapter V
Vaseline Glass from Europe

Canary opalescent and cranberry seven lily epergne, c. 1880s-90s. The bowl of this beautiful European epergne is cranberry on the outside cased with opal on the inside. Notice the unusual shape of three of the lilies. 23.63"h x 12"d. $3000-3200. *Courtesy of Kelvin Russell and Debra Jennings.*

Bohemian floraform vase with cranberry around the fluted edge, c. 1880-1900. 7"h x 10.75"d x 5.25"b. $700-900. *Courtesy of Melanie Schonier.*

Bohemian vase, c. early 1900s. The body of this beautiful ribbed vase is Vaseline and richly decorated with hand painted flowers and leaves in bright colors of pink and white plus blue and white with yellow centers and gold stems. The applied Vaseline leaf twining around the vase has purple highlights. 11.5"h x 5"d. $375-400. *Courtesy of Catherine F. Conrady.*

Bohemian *Jack-in-the-Pulpit* vase possibly by Moser, c. early 1900s. This beautiful opalescent stripe vase with gold flowers is 21"h x 6.5"b. $1800-2000. *Collection of Frank, Melissa, & Laura Keathley "Top Shelf Antiques."*

Czech console set. A wheel cut console bowl and candlesticks with a bird and flower design silver overlay. Made in Czechoslovakia, c. 1930s. Bowl, 4"h x 12"d. Candlesticks, 8.25"h x 4"b. $400-450 set. *Courtesy of Merle Pfannenstiel.*

Czech bowl made by Kralik, c. 1930s. This Vaseline bowl has millefiori caning and random blue threading. 3.5"h x 6.75"d. $100-150. *Courtesy of Melanie Schonier.*

96   Vaseline Glass from Europe

Czech vase by Kralic, c. 1930s. This Vaseline vase has millefiori caning, random cobalt threading, and tomato red and Vaseline applied handles. It is acid etched "Czechoslovakia." 6.5"h x 6"w excluding handles. $275-325. *Courtesy of Melanie Schonier.*

Czech water set by Kralik, c. 1930s. This 8.5"h bulbous Vaseline pitcher with applied handle and the 5.5"h tumblers have random orange threading and millefiori caning. All pieces are acid etched "Czechoslovakia." $500-575 set. *Courtesy of Melanie Schonier.*

Vaseline Glass from Europe 97

Czech vase, c. 1930s. This mold blown vase is marked on the bottom with acid etch "Czechoslovakia." The base glass is clear Vaseline with leaf-like decoration in contrasting red and orange. 7.5"h x 6"d. $350-400. *Courtesy of Melanie Schonier.*

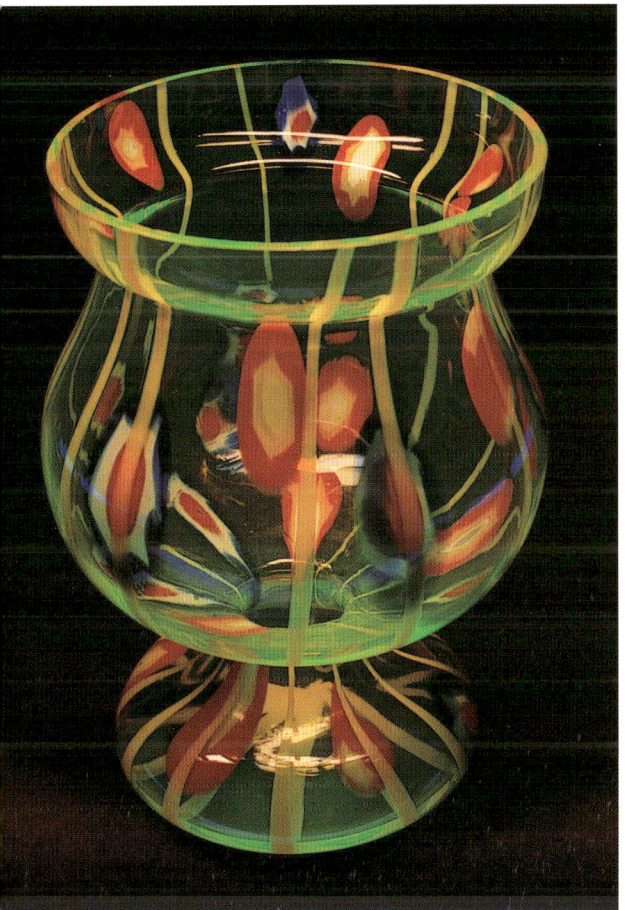

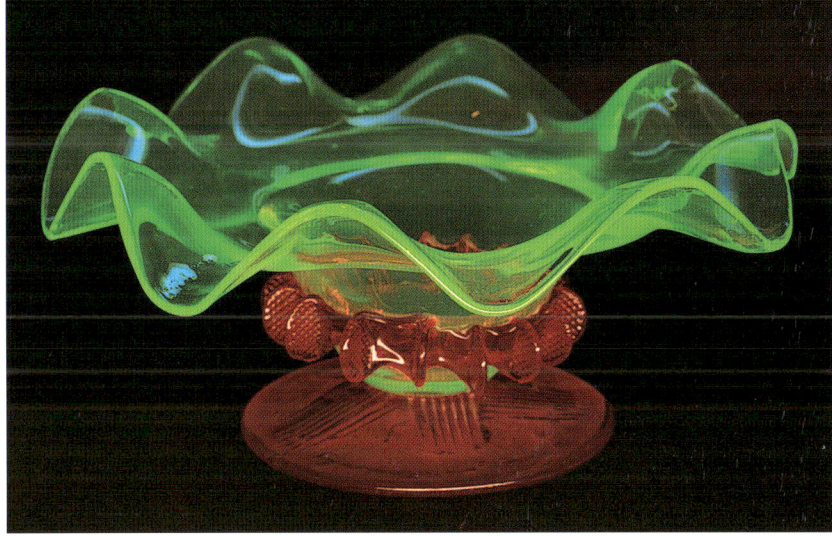

Footed Czech bowl, c. 1930s. This Czechoslovakian Vaseline bowl with ruby foot and rigaree bears the original paper label. 4"h x 9"d. $300-375. *Courtesy of Melanie Schonier.*

Czech vase by Kralik, c. 1930s. A furnace decorated vase with random striping and millefiori canes. 5.75"h x 4"d. $175-225. *Courtesy of Melanie Schonier.*

98 Vaseline Glass from Europe

Czech vase, c. 1920s. This paneled Vaseline vase has red windings and four orange prunts. 6"h x 4.83"d. $250-300. *Courtesy of Melanie Schonier.*

Czech mold blown vase, c. 1920-30s. This attractive vase is furnace decorated with tomato red applied handles and windings. 8.5"h. $150-175. *Courtesy of Melanie Schonier.*

Czech vase, c. 1930s. This vase has a reverse swirl Vaseline body with a fused red foot. 7"h x 4.1"b. $150-175. *Courtesy of Melanie Schonier.*

Vaseline Glass from Europe 99

Czech vase made by Kralik, c. 1930s. The mold blown vase is marked on the bottom in acid etch "Czechoslovakia." It is furnace decorated with an orange spiral drape design. 7.25"h x 3.75"b. $225-250. *Courtesy of Melanie Schonier.*

A Czech reverse swirl, mold blown vase with red applied handles, c. 1930s. 6.25"h x 4.3"b. $150-175. *Courtesy of Melanie Schonier.*

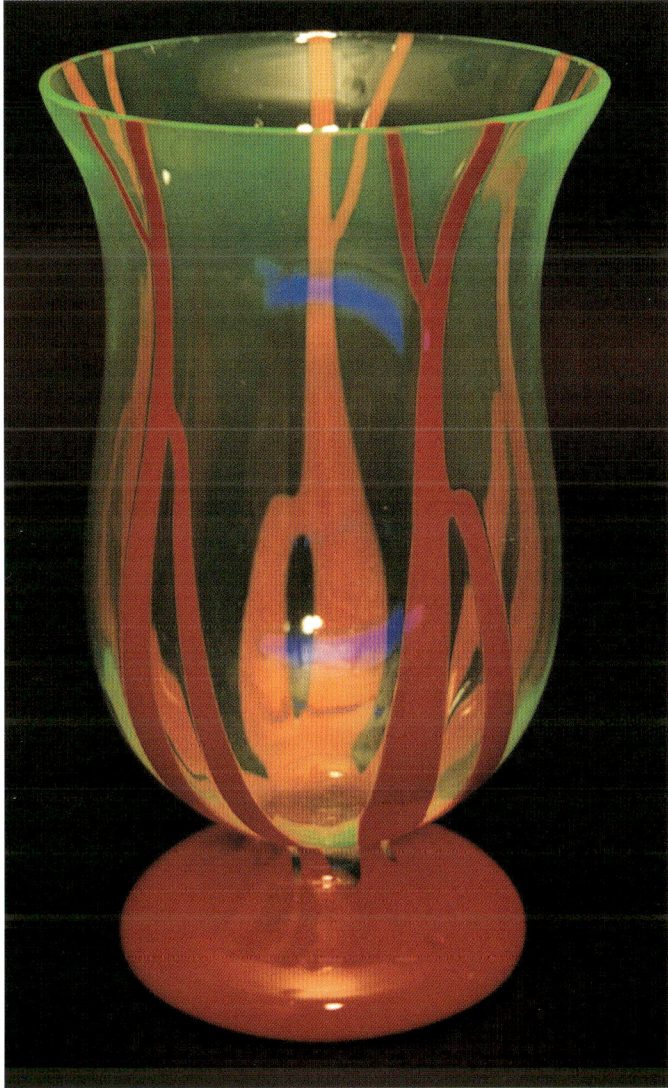

Czech vase, possibly Kralik, marked on the bottom with acid etch "Czechoslovakia," c. 1930s. The base glass of this typical furnace decorated Czech vase is Vaseline, with red glass applied to the base and extended to the top. 8.25"h x 4.88"d x 3.87"b. $300-350. *Courtesy of Bill McFarling.*

100   Vaseline Glass from Europe

Czech vase, c. 1930s. This blue and red mottle Czechoslovakian vase is cased in Vaseline. Under normal light this vase just looks blue with red spots. The Vaseline is not noticeable until it is under black light so be sure to test a piece like this before purchasing it as Vaseline. 11"h x 4.25"b. $225-250. *Courtesy of Melanie Schonier.*

Czech basket by Kralik, c. 1930s. This mold blown Vaseline basket has red, white, and blue millefiori caning with red windings and a ground and polished pontil. 9"h x 7.25"l x 6.5"w. $300-350. *Courtesy of Melanie Schonier.*

Czech basket by Kralik, c. 1930s. A rare Czechoslovakian mottled blue and red basket with Vaseline Glass overlay and applied red and Vaseline handle. 7.25"h x 6"l x 4"w. $275-325. *Courtesy of Melanie Schonier.*

Czech basket possibly by Kralik, c. 1930s. This Vaseline floraform basket with ruby edging and handle has a ground pontil. 11"h x 7"l x 5.25"w. $275-325. *Courtesy of Melanie Schonier.*

Vaseline Glass from Europe 101

Crackle glass pitcher, possibly Czech, c. 1920s-1930s. This blown pitcher with applied, twisted, and reeded handle is 8"h x 6"d. $125-175. *Courtesy of Melanie Schonier.*

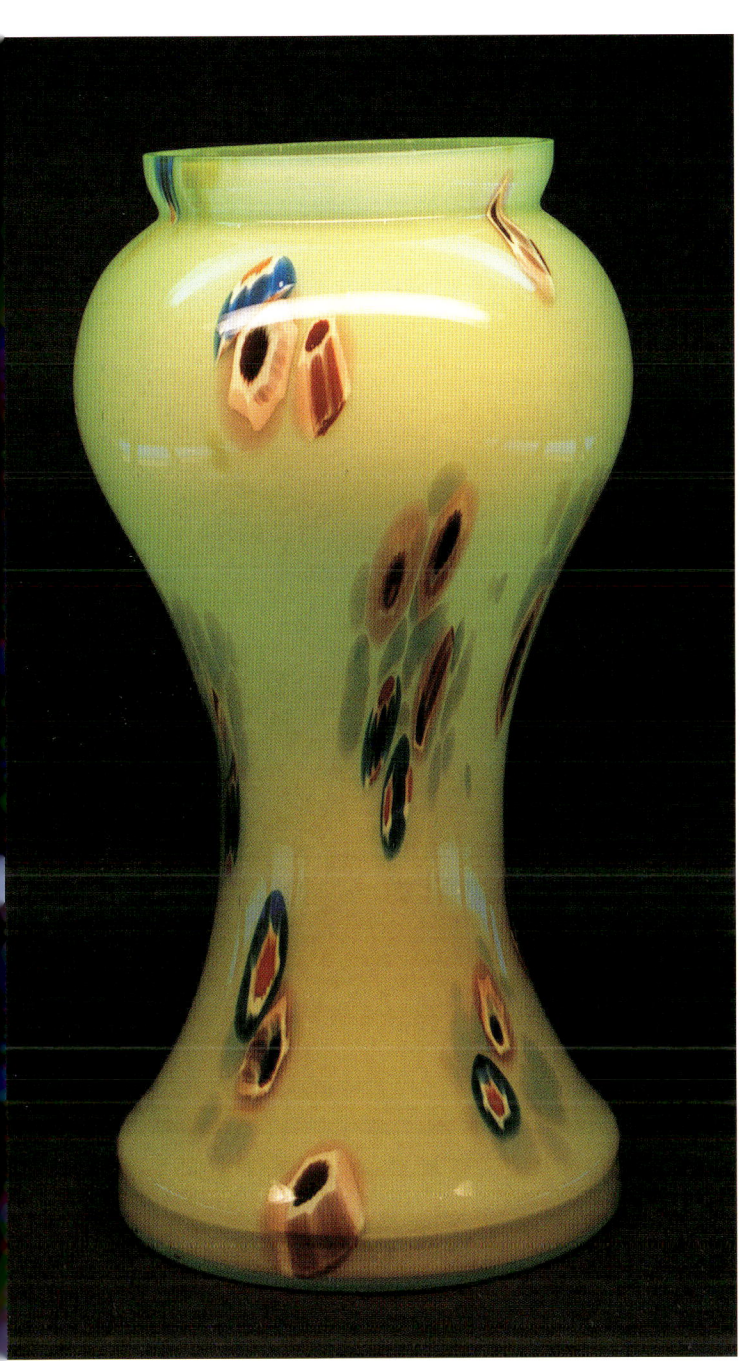

Czech vase, possibly by Kralik, c. 1930s. This Vaseline cased vase with two different color combinations of millefiori caning is acid etched "Czechoslovakia." 11.1"h x 5.25"b. $250-300. *Courtesy of Melanie Schonier.*

Czech crackle glass pitcher, c. 1920-30s. 9.75"h. $175-200.

Vaseline Glass from Europe

Czech bowl, c. 1920-30s. This threaded bowl is acid etched "Czechoslovakia" on the bottom and is very light in color. 2.45"h x 4.75"d. $15-20. *Courtesy of Bill McFarling.*

A miniature perfume with jewels and ormolu produced in Czechoslovakia, c. 1930s. You will only be able to see the top glow on this little purse perfume. $225-275. *Courtesy of Melanie Schonier.*

Bohemian long stem cut crystal cordials, c. 1880s-90s. 5.9"h. $50-65 ea.

Czech cut glass bowl. 3"h x 5.4"d. $150-175.

Czech pin tray by Heinrick Hoffmann, c. 1930s. The identifying pressed butterfly mark can be seen in the right lower corner. These pieces are sometimes referred to as Intaglio salts. 0.75"h x 2.75"l x 2"w. $65-75. *Courtesy of Catherine F. Conrady.*

Vaseline Glass from Europe 103

Bohemian floraform pedestal vase, c. 1920s. $100-125. *Courtesy of Catherine F. Conrady.*

Bohemian basket, c. 1890s. The Vaseline top of this pink basket resembles four leaves, with the back two folding up to form the handle. 6"h x 3.4"d. $150-175. *Courtesy of Catherine F. Conrady.*

A pink vase with hand applied canary top and white frit decoration. Possibly Bohemian, c. 1880s-90s. 4"h x 3.8"d. $175-200. *Courtesy of Kelvin Russell and Debra Jennings.*

Bohemian basket, c, 1890s. The twisted, applied handle is typical of the period. The edge is deep rose and crimped. Only the handle and leaves are Vaseline. 6.25"h x 5.8"d. $175-225. *Courtesy of Lena Lou Staton.*

Opalescent swirl art glass basket shading to peach with a looped handle and leaves in canary and a yellow applied flower. European, c. 1880s-90s. 6.5"h x 5.25"d. $175-195. *Courtesy of Kelvin Russell and Debra Jennings.*

Art glass canary baskets with ruffled pink colored tops. Possibly Stevens & Williams, c. 1890s. The large basket has a rope handle and measures 6.25"h x 8"d. $225-250. The small basket is 5.5"h x 4.75"d. $150-175. *Courtesy of Kelvin Russell and Debra Jennings.*

Vaseline Glass from Europe 105

A cranberry and white spatter Czech basket with hand applied canary opalescent decoration, c. 1917. 6.89"h x 4.6"l x 2.8"w x 3"b. $150-175.

Waffle basket, possibly Czech, c. 1917. The thorn handle is applied, the rim is white, and there is a wide opalescent band on the inside just below the crimped edge. 7.75"h x 7"d. $150-175. *Courtesy of Catherine F. Conrady.*

Art glass basket, possibly Stevens & Williams, c. 1890s. This beautiful purple opalescent stripe basket has a canary looped thorn handle and canary applied leaves and stems. The applied flower is yellow. 10"h. $325-375. *Courtesy of Cindy and Ben Burchfield.*

Art glass basket, possibly English, c. 1880-90s. This blown, paneled basket has bubbles contained throughout. The handle is looped and typical of the period. The fluted edge is cranberry. 6.75"h x 6.65"d. $175-225. *Courtesy of Lena Lou Staton.*

Vaseline Glass from Europe 107

Czech basket, c. 1917. This basket has an amethyst bowl and a Vaseline hand applied crimped top and smooth handle. 7.75"h x 4.25"d. $125-150. *Courtesy of Keri Davis.*

Rose bowl, possibly Bohemian, c. 1890s. This opalescent stripe pattern with applied flowers has also been attributed to Stevens & Williams of England and Hobbs, Brockunier of the U.S. Very similar wares were produced in all three areas in the same era, making definite attribution extremely difficult. 4.75"h x 5"d. $200-250. *Courtesy of W. C. "Red" Roetteis.*

Art glass basket, possibly Bohemian, c. 1890s. This opalescent stripe basket with applied Vaseline looped handle that becomes the stem of the cranberry and white flower is 6"h x 3.85"d. $200-250. *Courtesy of Catherine F. Conrady.*

European rose bowls, c. 1880s-90s. Canary *Stripe Optic* rose bowl with applied cranberry flowers and canary leaves. 3.37"h x 4.25"d. Canary *Lattice* rose bowl with applied cranberry flowers and clear leaves. 3.37"h x 4.4"d. $100-125 ea. *Courtesy of Kelvin Russell and Debra Jennings.*

A canary *Stripe Optic* rose bowl with blue enameled flowers. Possibly English, c. 1880s-90s. 3.2"h x 3.85"d. $100-125. *Courtesy of Kelvin Russell and Debra Jennings.*

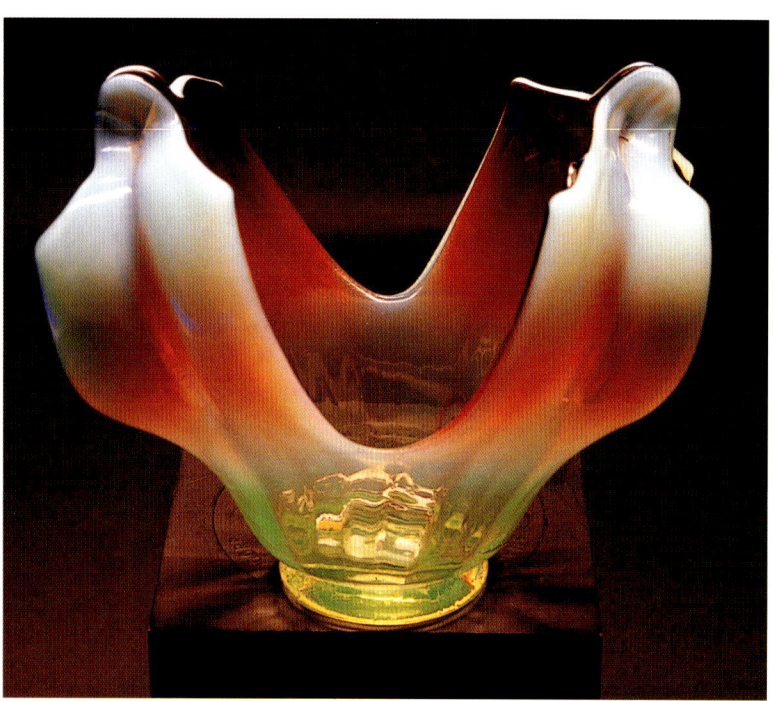

Pigeon Blood basket, possibly English, c. 1880-90s. This double handle basket has opalescence on the outside of the leaf shaped handles and dark blood red on the inside. 4.75"h x 5.5"l x 3.75"w. $175-200. *Courtesy of Catherine F. Conrady.*

A *Horse Chestnut* canary opalescent vase by Richardsons of Wordsley, England, c. 1916. 3.25"h x 3"d. $140-160. *Courtesy of Kelvin Russell and Debra Jennings.*

Vaseline Glass from Europe 109

Jack-in-the-Pulpit Vaseline vase with cranberry top, gold decoration, and white flowers. European, c. 1880s-90s. 5.5"h x 4"d. $160-180. *Courtesy of Kelvin Russell and Debra Jennings.*

A highly enameled opal vase cased in Vaseline, with applied amber feet. European, c. 1880s-90s. 7"h x 4.75"d. $250-280. *Courtesy of Kelvin Russell and Debra Jennings.*

Jack-in-the-Pulpit vase, possibly English, c. 1890s. This purple blown *Jack-in-the-Pulpit* vase has opalescent stripes. The applied feet and leaves are canary, the flower is yellow. 6.5"h x 3.5"d. $225-275. *Courtesy of Cindy and Ben Burchfield.*

A 5-footed, opalescent, swirl pattern, art glass vase shading to purple. Possibly English, c. 1880s-90s. 7"h. $150-175. *Courtesy of Kelvin Russell and Debra Jennings.*

Lattice canary opalescent art glass vases with applied cranberry flowers. European, c. 1880s-90s. 6.5"h x 4.15"w. $150-175 ea. *Courtesy of Kelvin Russell and Debra Jennings.*

An opalescent flower design English vase, possibly from the Stourbridge area, c. early 1900s. 4.5"h x 4.15"d. $100-125. *Courtesy of Kelvin Russell and Debra Jennings.*

Vaseline Glass from Europe 111

A pink *Lattice* ewer with canary applied decoration. English, c. 1880s-90s. 9"h x 3.5"d. $225-250. *Courtesy of Kelvin Russell and Debra Jennings.*

An art glass canary opalescent stripe vase with cranberry applied flowers. European, c. 1890s. 8.5"h x 4.1"b. $75-95. *Courtesy of Catherine F. Conrady.*

A pink opalescent art glass ewer, c. 1880s. The opalescence is in a lattice pattern and the leaves and stem decoration are Vaseline. 6.75"h x 3.35"d x 2.2"b. $100-125.

Jack-in-the-Pulpit vase, possibly English, c. late 1800s. This unusual blown vase has an opalescent top with a blue rim. 7"h x 4.5"b. $125-150. *Courtesy of Cindy and Ben Burchfield.*

Art glass vase, possibly English, c. 1880-90s. This very interesting Victorian era vase is paneled with opalescence at the top. The leaf applied at the right side of the 5-footed base holds another tiny clear vase (piece of paper inside looks pink for distinction). 6.1"h x 3.5"b. $175-195. *Courtesy of Catherine F. Conrady.*

Angel epergne, possibly English, c. late 1800s. This single lily epergne is very attractive with its swirl pattern, opalescent top, and angel base. 10.75"h, base 5"w. $250-275. *Courtesy of Cindy and Ben Burchfield.*

Vaseline Glass from Europe   113

An unusual light blue opalescent vase with canary base and windings. European, c. 1890s. 8"h. $95-125. *Courtesy of Catherine F. Conrady.*

Art glass vase, possibly Bohemian, c. 1880-90s. This cranberry vase has a canary ruffled top and has been seen in various sizes. 9"h x 3.5"b. $175-200. *Courtesy of Catherine F. Conrady.*

Art glass vase, possibly English, c. 1880-90s. This Vaseline opalescent vase shades to blue at the top. The base is clear Vaseline. 8"h x 3.25"b. $125-150. *Courtesy of Catherine F. Conrady.*

Jack-in-the-Pulpit vase, possibly English, c. 1880s. The canary shades to opalescence and cranberry. The rigaree has some cranberry on the little knobs where it is pinched. 7.75"h. $125-150. *Courtesy of Glen Cheatham, Jr.*

Jack-in-the-Pulpit vase, Bohemian, c. 1880-90s. This vase has a green top and mica inclusions (silver flecks). 10.75"h. $175-200. *Courtesy of Glen Cheatham, Jr.*

Vaseline Glass from Europe 115

Jack-in-the-Pulpit vase, English, c. 1880s. This vase shades from canary to opalescence and cranberry. 12.75"h. $175-200. *Courtesy of Glen Cheatham, Jr.*

Jack-in-the-Pulpit vase, English, c. 1880s. A canary vase shading from canary to opalescence and blue. 12.5"h. $175-200. *Courtesy of Glen Cheatham, Jr.*

116   Vaseline Glass from Europe

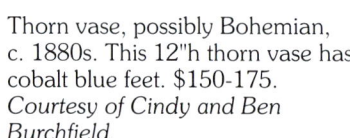

Thorn vase, possibly Bohemian, c. late 1800s. This unusual blown double thorn vase is white cased in Vaseline. 12"h x 4"b. $125-150. *Courtesy of Cindy and Ben Burchfield.*

Thorn vase, possibly Bohemian, c. 1880s. This 12"h thorn vase has cobalt blue feet. $150-175. *Courtesy of Cindy and Ben Burchfield.*

A large Vaseline vase with opalescent ribs and a Venini label, c. 1960s. 18.37"h x 7"b. $350-400. *Courtesy of Melanie Schonier.*

Vaseline Glass from Europe 117

Art glass 5-footed vase with opalescent cranberry top. European, c. 1880s-90s. 9.5"h x 4"b. $165-185. *Courtesy of Kelvin Russell and Debra Jennings.*

Jack-in-the-Pulpit satin, canary and cranberry, stripe, 5-footed vase by Thomas Webb, c. 1880s-90s. 12.5"h. $550-575. *Courtesy of Kelvin Russell and Debra Jennings.*

Opalescent swirl *Jack-in-the-Pulpit* vases with green edges. Possibly English, c. 1880s-90s. 10"h. $125-150 ea. *Courtesy of Kelvin Russell and Debra Jennings.*

Vaseline Glass from Europe 119

A tall cranberry art glass vase with Vaseline rigaree. Possibly English, c. 1880s-90s. 20.5"h x 5.75"b. $150-175. *Courtesy of Kelvin Russell and Debra Jennings.*

An English opalescent Daffodils vase, c. 1880s-90s. 9.75"h x 3.5"b. $170-180. *Courtesy of Kelvin Russell and Debra Jennings.*

120 Vaseline Glass from Europe

Single lily epergne, possibly English, c. 1880s. This epergne has a leaf design holder. The canary lily shades to opalescent, with a green rim and green plating inside the top and applied canary rigaree. 10.5"h. $150-175. *Courtesy of Catherine F. Conrady.*

Lilypad epergne, possibly English, c. 1880-90s. The base of this epergne is in the shape of a lilypad. The leaves are gold and the flower bud is Vaseline. The two horns with rigaree are Vaseline with opalescent ruffled tops. 11"h, base is 12"l x 8.5"w. $250-300. *Courtesy of Cindy and Ben Burchfield.*

A five lily canary opalescent epergne, possibly English, c. 1890s. These epergnes were also referred to as flower centerpieces. 11"h x 12"d. $900-950. *Courtesy of Cindy and Ben Burchfield.*

Vaseline Glass from Europe 121

Victorian bride's basket, possibly English, c. 1880s. Stand, 10.5"h. Bowl, 10.5"d. *Courtesy of Catherine F. Conrady.*

Pedestal bowl, English, c. 1880s. This opalescent swirl bowl has a ruffled and crimped edge with a cranberry rim. The Victorian figural silver plate pedestal is marked Simpson Hall Miller and Co. Treble Plate. 14"h x 11"d. $1100-1200. *Courtesy of Melanie Schonier.*

Bohemian flower centerpiece by Pallme Koenig with marquetry applied flower application, c. 1900-1910. The applied flower and stem are purple and there is a thin purple trim on the edges of the bowl and lily. There are hand painted flowers on the bottom side of the bowl. 15"h x 9.5"d. $600-700. *Courtesy of Cindy and Ben Burchfield.*

Rubina Verde compote, possibly English, c. late1800s. The silver plate base of this compote has a wooden stem. 7.75"h x 11"d. $250-275. *Courtesy of Cindy and Ben Burchfield.*

Vaseline Glass from Europe 123

Bride's bowl, possibly English, c. 1890s. The bowl of this piece has a waffle pattern and the canary shades to opalescence and blue. The stand is pot metal. 12"h x 10"d. $225-250. *Courtesy of Glen Cheatham, Jr.*

Pigeon Blood flower centerpiece, possibly English, c. 1890s. This beautiful epergne or flower centerpiece shades from canary to opalescence to pigeon blood (ox blood). 16"h x 11.5"d. $750-800. *Courtesy of Glen Cheatham, Jr.*

The owner of this piece believes it to be a marriage. It is pictured to alert the reader as to what can be found in the marketplace. A very attractive piece regardless. *Courtesy of Glen Cheatham, Jr.*

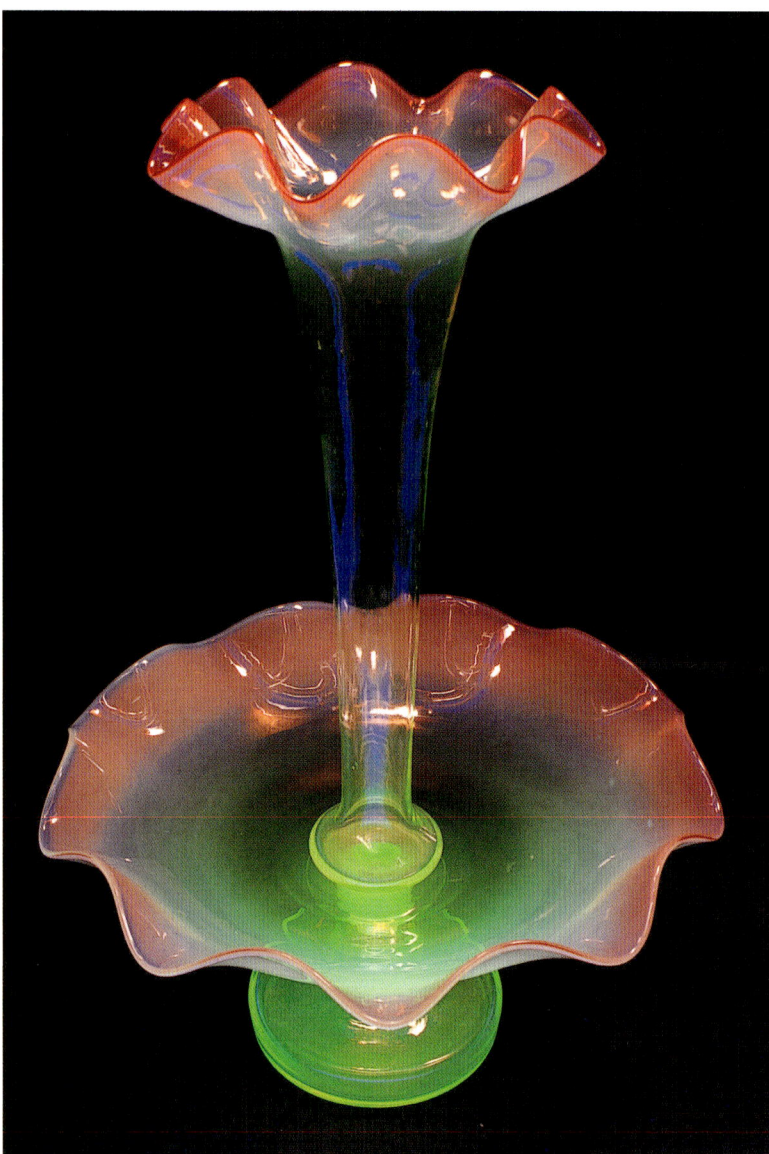

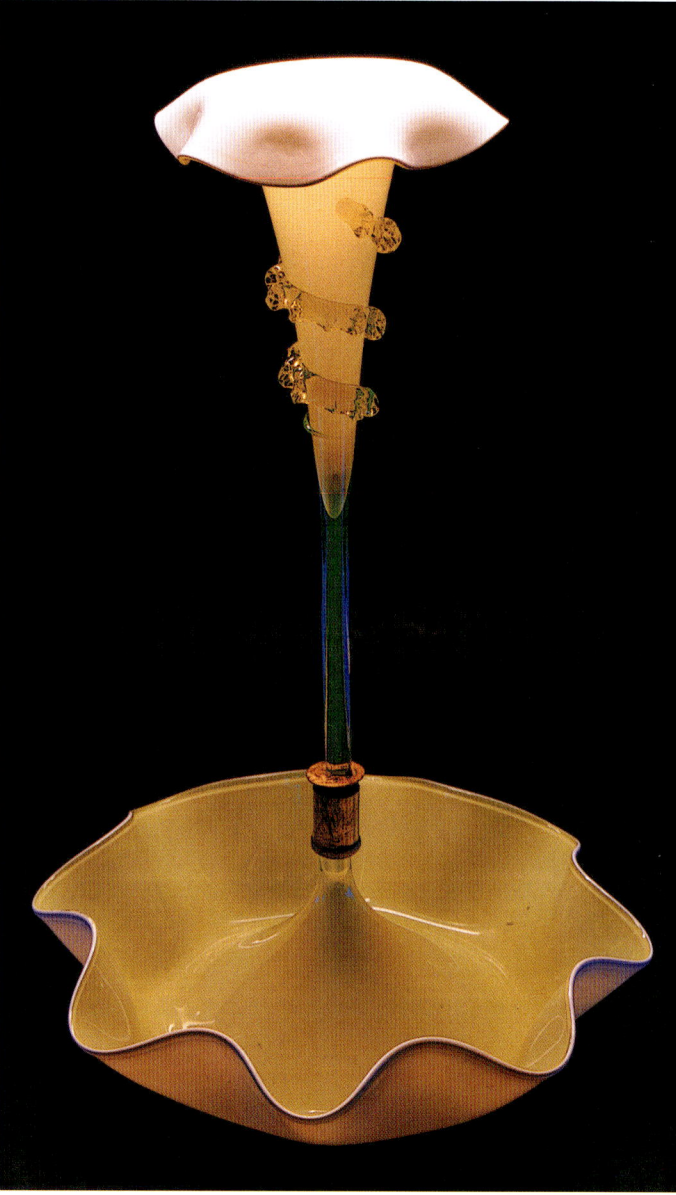

Epergne, possibly English, c. 1890s. This single lily canary epergne shades to opalescence and cranberry. These epergnes were also referred to as flower centerpieces. The bowl was used for fruit and the lily for flowers. 16"h x 10.25"d. $400-450. *Courtesy of Melanie Schonier.*

Single lily epergne, European, c. 1880s. An unusual piece, the bowl of this epergne is opal plated with canary on the inside; the lily is canary plated with opal on the inside. The applied rigaree is canary. You will only notice the fluorescence in the stem of the lily and the rigaree due to lighting. 14"h x 9"d. $400-450. *Courtesy of Glen Cheatham, Jr.*

Vaseline Glass from Europe 125

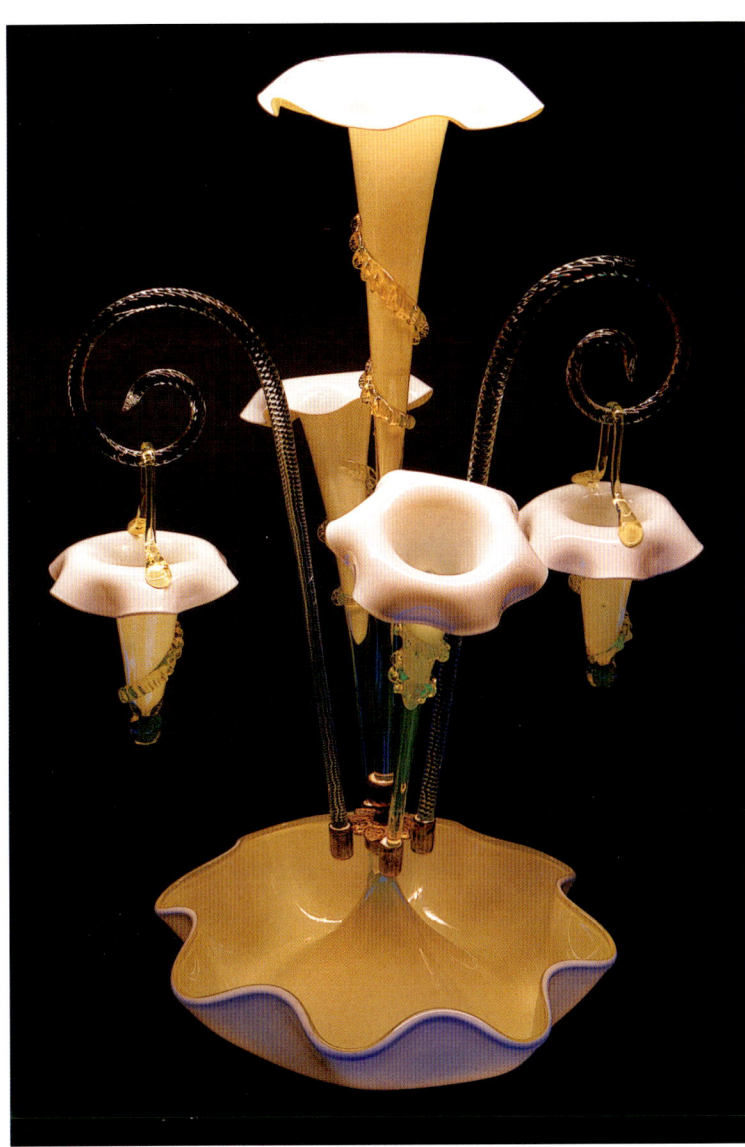

A more elaborate version of the previous epergne, European, c.1880s. The three lilies and two baskets are canary plated with opal on the inside, the applied rigaree (chaining) is canary, the canes are crystal, the base is opal cased with canary on the inside, very pretty. 21"h x 10.75"b. Basket, 6.5"l x 4.3"d. $1200-1500. *Courtesy of Catherine F. Conrady.*

Art glass bowl, possibly English, c. 1890s. This cranberry bowl has applied flower, stems, and feet in Vaseline and a sterling silver band with an English hallmark. $600-800. *Collection of Frank, Melissa, & Laura Keathley "Top Shelf Antiques."*

Venetian figural bowl and underplate, c. 1890-1900s. This beautiful set is paneled. The swan's head, body, and wings have gold inclusions. The eyes are black. The handles are not Vaseline. Plate, 7.25"d. Bowl, 2.5"h x 4.5"d. $250-300 set. *Courtesy of Melanie Schonier.*

Venetian stems. See description in preceding caption for bowl and underplate. Cordial, 5.25"h x 2.45"d x 2.5"b. $150-200. Wine, 7.5"h x 3.6"d x 4.8"b. $225-275. Champagne, 5.5"h x 7.65"d x 3.35"b. $225-275. *Courtesy of Melanie Schonier.*

Vaseline Glass from Europe 127

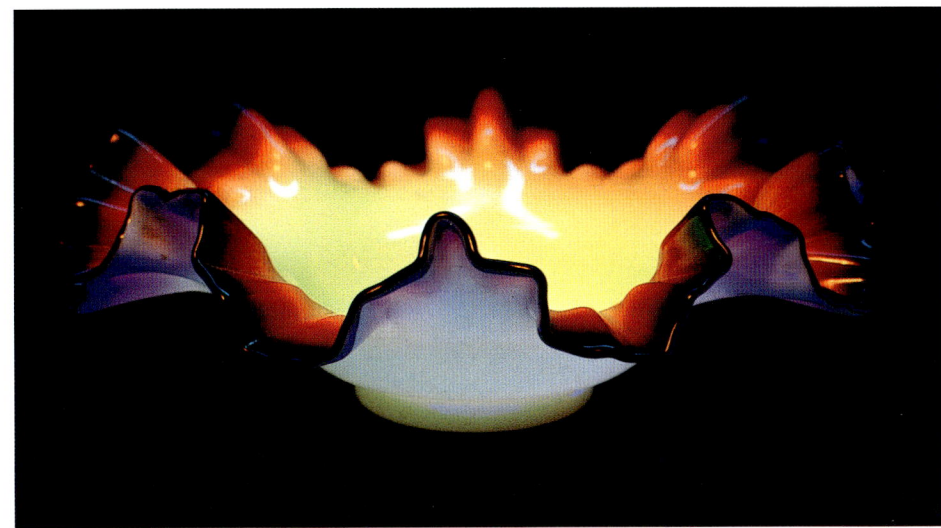

Victorian bowl, possibly English, c. 1880-90s. This bowl is white, plated with a canary interior. The crimped and ruffled edge is ruby. 2.5"h x 7.75"d. $100-125. *Courtesy of Melanie Schonier.*

Condiment set, c. 1880s. The top of this Thousand Eye insert is opalescent with a green rim. There is a Vaseline rigaree around the bowl that is difficult to see. The stand is electroplate nickel silver. 6"h. $300-325. *Courtesy of Melanie Schonier.*

Sweetmeat, possibly English, c. 1880-90s. A blue sweetmeat with canary rigaree around the center and a hand applied canary pinched top. Bowl, 3"h x 4.2"d. Holder, 5.5"h. $175-225. *Courtesy of Catherine F. Conrady.*

Sweetmeat, English, c. 1880s. This threaded canary opalescent sweetmeat has clear rigaree and a ground and polished pontil. 2"h x 5"d. The square engraved stand is silver plate, 5.25"h x 5.75"sq. $350-400. *Courtesy of Melanie Schonier.*

Sweetmeat, possibly English, c. 1880s. The fluted canary opalescent bowl with applied rigaree around the center has a ground and polished pontil. 2.25"h x 5"d. The ball footed frame is marked "Armour Brand" EPNS (electroplate nickel silver). 6.25"h x 6"w. $350-400. *Courtesy of Melanie Schonier.*

Sweetmeat, possibly English, c. 1880-90s. The canary opalescent bowl is very similar to the previously described bowl except for the shape of the top. 3"h x 5.25"d. The frame is marked EPNS. 6.65"h x 6.65"d. $350-400. *Courtesy of Melanie Schonier.*

Vaseline Glass from Europe 129

Double sweetmeat, possibly English, c. 1880-90s. The two threaded cranberry sweetmeats have fluted edges, double canary rigaree, and ground and polished pontils. 2.5"h x 5"d. The silver plate frame is 8"h. $400-475. *Courtesy of Melanie Schonier.*

Victorian bowl, possibly English, c. 1880-90s. This bowl is clear at the bottom and blue at the top. It has canary rigaree and a hand applied canary pinched top. The pontil is ground and polished. 2.75"h x 4"d. $150-175. *Courtesy of Melanie Schonier.*

Victorian bowl, possibly English, c. 1880-90s. This canary bowl with applied rigaree is trimmed in aqua. 3"h x 5.6"d. $150-175. *Courtesy of Lena Lou Staton.*

Vaseline Glass from Europe

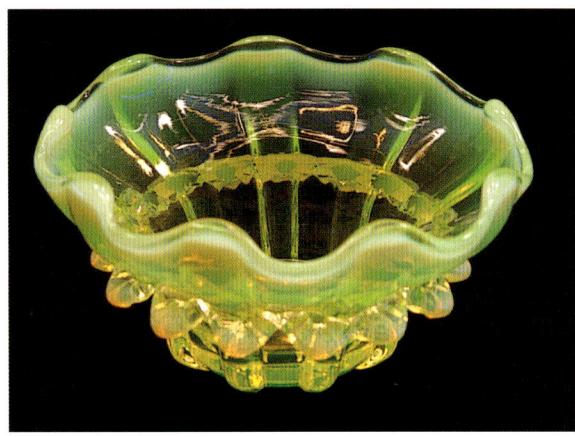

English salt, c. 1880s. This small canary salt with applied rigaree shades to opalescent at the ruffled top. Holder is missing. 1.5"h x 3"d. $125-150. *Courtesy of Catherine F. Conrady.*

A cranberry sweetmeat with opal windings and canary rigaree. English, c. 1880s-90s. 2.37"h x 5.5"d. $150-175. *Courtesy of Kelvin Russell and Debra Jennings.*

English open salt, c. 1880s. This canary open salt has a pointed, crimped edge, canary rigaree decoration, and a ground and polished pontil. The silver stand has repoussé grape and vine decoration and dolphin feet. 1.25"h x 3"d. $375-425. *Courtesy of Melanie Schonier.*

Canary drapery pattern sweetmeat with cranberry rim. English, c. 1880s-90s. Frame, 6.25"h. Insert, 3"h x 5"d. $225-250. *Courtesy of Kelvin Russell and Debra Jennings.*

Vaseline Glass from Europe 131

English open salts, c. 1880s. An assortment of canary opalescent open salts with rigaree decoration. The footed stands are all marked "EPNS," electroplated nickel silver. 1.25"h x 3"d. $250-350 ea. *Courtesy of Melanie Schonier.*

An illustration of the berry "signature" on the pontil of the salt on the right in the preceding photo. The finishing details often identify the artist.

English open salts, c. 1880s. A group of canary opalescent open salts with rigaree decoration. The footed stands are marked "EPNS." 1.25"h x 3"d. $250-350 ea. *Courtesy of Melanie Schonier.*

Violet vase, possibly English, c. 1880s. The basket vase of this beautiful piece is cranberry opalescent. The handle and stand are canary. Stand, 7"h. Basket, 4.5"h x 3"d. $500-575. *Courtesy of Catherine F. Conrady.*

Rubina Verde pitcher, possibly Thomas Webb & Son, c. 1890s. This extremely fine pitcher has hand painted white flowers. Matching cups complete this set. 6.75"h x 5.75"d. $1000-1200. *Collection of Frank, Melissa, & Laura Keathley "Top Shelf Antiques."*

Vaseline Glass from Europe 133

Berry set, possibly English, c. 1880-90s. This footed thumbprint pattern berry set has ground and polished pontils with prunts. Master berry, 4.25"h x 9"d. Small berry, 1.5"h x 4"d. $225-275 set. *Courtesy of Melanie Schonier.*

Double handled basket, possibly English, c. possibly 1900s. The edge of this basket is braided like a rope. Help with identification would be appreciated. 6.5"l x 6.25"w. $60-80.

English fairy light, c. early 1900s. This piece is marked S. CLARKS TRADE. MARK. PYRAMID. The base is Vaseline satin glass. The dome is clear satin glass but looks pink due to lighting. 6"h x 4.5"b. $175-200. *Courtesy of Catherine F. Conrady.*

134 Vaseline Glass from Europe

An English *Hobnail* cologne bottle, c. 1875. The marking on the bottom dates the piece. 5.35"h x 1.9"sq. $125-150. *Courtesy of Kelvin Russell and Debra Jennings.*

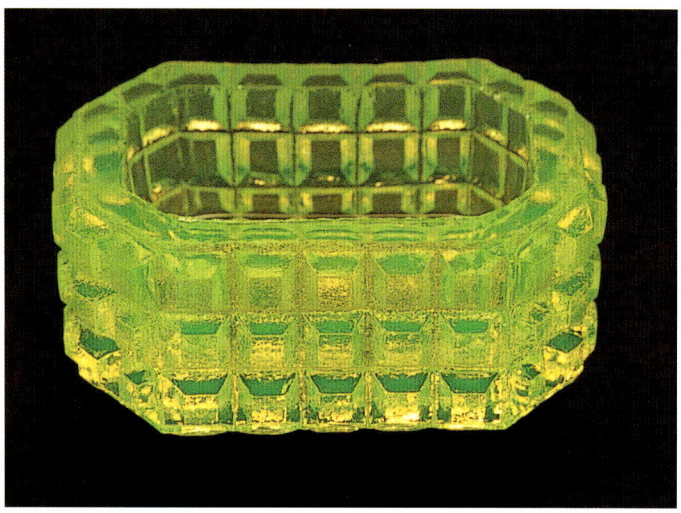

Block or *Waffle* pattern canary salt, possibly English, c. 1880-90s. 0.95"h x 2.35"l x 1.7"w. $50-60. *Courtesy of Catherine F. Conrady.*

English pressed glass basket by Greener & Co., c. 1872. 3.5"h x 4.85"l x 4"w. $50-75.

Quilted Daisy fairy lamp by Greener & Co., c. 1890s. The registry number of this pattern is Rd 176239. Greener, a competitor of George Davidson, produced Pearline for only a short time. Consequently Greener's Pearline items are rarer than Davidson's and have a higher market value. 4.5"h x 5"d. $425-475. *Courtesy of Dennis and Marilyn Tuttle.*

Vaseline Glass from Europe 135

Conch and Twig wall pocket by Burtles, Tate & Co., Rd 39807, Jan. 8, 1885. This Uranium Topas Opalescent (Vaseline) wall pocket is 7.75"l x 3.6"w. $250-275.

Brideshead celery by George Davidson & Sons, Rd 130641, 8/13/1889. 7"h x 5.4"d. $320-350. *Courtesy of John C. Bell.*

136 Vaseline Glass from Europe

Sowerby "Pearline," Pattern No. 1254.5. Registered Sept. 18, 1877. This is an English salt and the design registration is based on the letters and numbers in the four points of a diamond on the bottom of the piece. 1.75"h x 2.75"d. $ 125-150.

Lady Caroline Pearline Primrose baskets by George Davidson & Co. c. 1891. The three handled basket measures 3.25"h x 3.75"d. The two handled basket measures 3"h x 4"d. $90-110 ea. *Courtesy of John C. Bell.*

War of Roses bowls by George Davidson & Co., Rd 212684, 5/25/1893. Two different bowl shapes are pictured, a three prong and a four prong. Davidson's name for this Vaseline opalescent color was "Primrose Pearline." Pearline refers to the opalescent treatment. Davidson patented this process. Four prong bowl, 1.5"h x 5"d. Three prong bowl, 1.5"h x 3.5"d. $190-220 ea. *Courtesy of John C. Bell.*

Lady Caroline spills (vases). The heavy opalescence of these *Primrose Pearline* spills is typical of English opalescent glass. Tall spill, 4.75"h x 1.75"d. $150-175. Short spill, 3.75"h x 2"d, $100-125. *Courtesy of John C. Bell.*

Vaseline Glass from Europe 137

English vase, possibly by Greener & Co., c. 1890s. 5"h x 3.75"d. $160-180.

Lady Caroline Pearline Primrose sugar and creamer. Sugar, 2"h x 3.75"d. $75-90. Creamer, 2.5"h x 2.75"d. $80-100. *Courtesy of John C. Bell.*

Victoria and Albert tazza by George Davidson & Co., Rd 303519, 8/18/1897. The registry number can be found in the bottom of the plate. Two views of this tazza (small cake stand) are shown for pattern detail. 3.25"h x 8"d. $270-290. *Courtesy of John C. Bell.*

Lords and Ladies sugar and nappy by George Davidson & Co., Rd 285342, 10/2/1896. The sugar at the top measures 4.5"h x 5"d. $180-200. The nappy measures 1.25"h x 5.5"l x 4"d. $180-200. *Courtesy of John C. Bell.*

Victoria and Albert open sugar and nappy. John Bell of England related that the sugar bowls of this period were large because the sugar was not refined. The large open sugar at the top measures 5.25"h x 6"d. $200-230. The nappy on the bottom measures 1.25"h x 5.75"l x 4.25"w. $150-175. *Courtesy of John C. Bell.*

English creamers. The *Lords and Ladies* creamer on the left measures 3"h x 2.5"d. $150-175. The *Lady Caroline* creamer on the right measures 2"h x 2"d. $80-100. *Courtesy of John C. Bell.*

Vaseline Glass from Europe   139

English creamers by George Davidson & Co. John Bell of England named the creamer on the left *"Helen Louise,"* c. 1890s. 3.75"h x 2.5"d. $75-90. The center creamer is *Somerset*, Rd 254027, 5/1/1895. 5"h x 2.75"d. $260-280. The creamer on the right is *William and Mary*, Rd 413701, 7/14/1903. 3.25"h x 2.75"d. $90-110. *Courtesy of John C. Bell.*

English nappies by George Davidson & Co. On the left *Prince William*, Rd. 217752, 10/6/1893. 1.25"h x 6.5"l x 4.75"w. $140-160. On the right *Linking Rings*, Rd 237038, 8/1/1894. 1.25"h x 5.37"l x 4.25"w. $115-125. *Courtesy of John C. Bell.*

Lords and Ladies open sugar, 3"h x 4.75"d. $140-160. *Courtesy of John C. Bell.*

War of Roses bowl by George Davidson & Co., Rd 212684, 5/25/1893. This bowl was made in three sizes. A smaller version is pictured in *The Picture Book of Vaseline Glass*, pg. 139. 8"l x 2"w. $145-175.

Quilted Pillow Sham by George Davidson & Co., c. 1890. There is no registry number on this covered butter. 4"h x 7"l x 5.5"w. $300-350.

A block pattern cologne and powder box, possibly French, c. 1930s. Cologne, 5.6"h x 2.3"d. Powder box, 4.1"h x 2.4"d. $75-85 set. *Courtesy of Bruce P. Schiwitz.*

French Baccarat swirl pattern cologne bottle. Production date unknown. 6.5"h x 2.75"d. $150-200. *Courtesy of Catherine F. Conrady.*

Vaseline Glass from Europe 141

A swirl pattern dish, possibly French. Production date unknown. 1.35"h x 4.8"l x 3.65"w. $45-55. *Courtesy of Catherine F. Conrady.*

A vanity box, possibly English, c. 1880s. 5"h x 3.1"d. $125-150. *Courtesy of Cindy and Ben Burchfield.*

French vanity set, c. 1890s-early 1900s. This vanity set is marked Verreries De Scailmont Manace. In *The Picture Book of Vaseline Glass*, the author named this pattern *Zippered Star*. I still have not been able to determine the original pattern name. Small puff box, 3"h x 2.9"d. $75-85. Bowl, 2.6"h x 5"l x 3.65"w. $55-65. Large puff box, 3.75"h x 2.9"d. $85-95. *Courtesy of Catherine F. Conrady.*

Small jewelry box, possibly Austrian, c. 1880-90s. The following wording is on the lid "Bad Nauheim, Korhaus." 2.25"h x 3"l x 2.5"w. $125-150. *Courtesy of Cindy and Ben Burchfield.*

A French seltzer bottle, c. 1920s. The cap reads *Etablissements Vigneron*. The bottle reads *E TABL. VIGNERON, +LA GARENNE+*. 12.75"h. $225-250. *Courtesy of Catherine F. Conrady.*

142 Vaseline Glass from Europe

Daisy decanter or vase by Riihlmaen Lasi, Finland, c. 1970s. 9.25"h x 6.75"w. $50-75. *Courtesy of Catherine F. Conrady.*

Vaseline wine glass, possibly German, c. 1920s. The glass has etched flowers on the bowl and a threaded stem. 7"h. $125-150. *Courtesy of Cindy and Ben Burchfield.*

Flint glass goblet with "MAABLIOBCHOE" on the bottom. It is believed to be Russian, c. 1850s. 6"h x 3.25"d. $350-400. *Courtesy of Beverly Scherer.*

A European bowl and underplate, possibly Monot Stumpf, c. early 1900s. This clear opalescent striped bowl and underplate have machine threading. There is a hint of gold on the threading. The crimped edges of the bowl and plate are Vaseline. The pontil is ground smooth. Bowl, 2.5"h x 6"d. Plate 1"h x 7"d. $250-275. *Courtesy of Catherine F. Conrady.*

Vaseline Glass from Europe 143

A miniature pitcher produced by Bimini Werkstatte in Vienna, Austria between 1923-1938. Bimini glass is characterized by its feather-lightness. 2.5"h. $80-100. *Courtesy of Melanie Schonier.*

Buddha trinket box, made in Austria, c. 1930s. The top is cut Vaseline, the bottom is black. 4.75"h x 4.4"l x 3.4"w. $250-350. *Collection of Frank, Melissa, & Laura Keathley "Top Shelf Antiques."*

French cameo vase with floral motif and gilt decoration, possibly by Mont Joye or Val St. Lambert, c. 1880s. The flowers, leaves, and stems are green trimmed in gold. 5.25"h. $375-425. *Courtesy of Melanie Schonier.*

French cameo perfume by Val St Lambert, c. early 1900s. This signed perfume is emerald green cut to Vaseline. 10.25"h x 4"b. $1800-2000. *Collection of Frank, Melissa, & Laura Keathley "Top Shelf Antiques."*

French cameo vase by Val St Lambert, c. early 1900s. This beautiful, signed vase is emerald green cut to Vaseline. 14.75"h x 4.75"b. $2200-2500. *Collection of Frank, Melissa, & Laura Keathley "Top Shelf Antiques."*

Cut glass wine decanter set, possibly Baccarat, c. early 1900s. The decanter is ruby cut to Vaseline, 17.5"h x 5.3"b. $1700-2000. One stem is orange cut to Vaseline, the other is ruby cut to Vaseline. 7.5"h. $200-300 ea. *Collection of Frank, Melissa, & Laura Keathley "Top Shelf Antiques."*

Vaseline Glass from Europe 145

Ikora bowl by German manufacturer WMF, c. 1930s. This Ikora glass bowl with orange inclusions is 2.25"h x 9.24"d. $150-200. *Courtesy of Melanie Schonier.*

Cut glass stem possibly Baccarat, c. early 1900s. This stem is blue cut to Vaseline. 7.5"h. $200-300. *Collection of Frank, Melissa, & Laura Keathley "Top Shelf Antiques."*

A stylized pig with brown shading at the base, possibly Scandinavian, c. 1950s. 3.1"h x 4.5"l x 2.45"w. $35-45. *Courtesy of Ben Curtis.*

Cut glass decanter and cordials, c. late 1800s-early 1900s. The silver top of the decanter has an English hallmark, but the glass may not be English. Decanter 8.5"h x 3.5"d. Cordial, 3.1"h x 2"d. $1700-2000 set. *Collection of Frank, Melissa, & Laura Keathley "Top Shelf Antiques."*

Vaseline Glass from Europe

Murano birds, c. 1950s. The Vaseline birds of this figural piece of Italian glass have brown heads. The base is clear. 11.5"h x 9"w. $200-250. *Courtesy of Melanie Schonier.*

Vaseline Murano figural fish with red sommerso and crystal bases, c. 1950s. 13.75"h x 3.3"b. $125-150 ea.

A ruby sommerso freeform Italian art glass lighter, c. 1950s. 4"h x 3.25"d. $100-110. *Courtesy of Bill McFarling.*

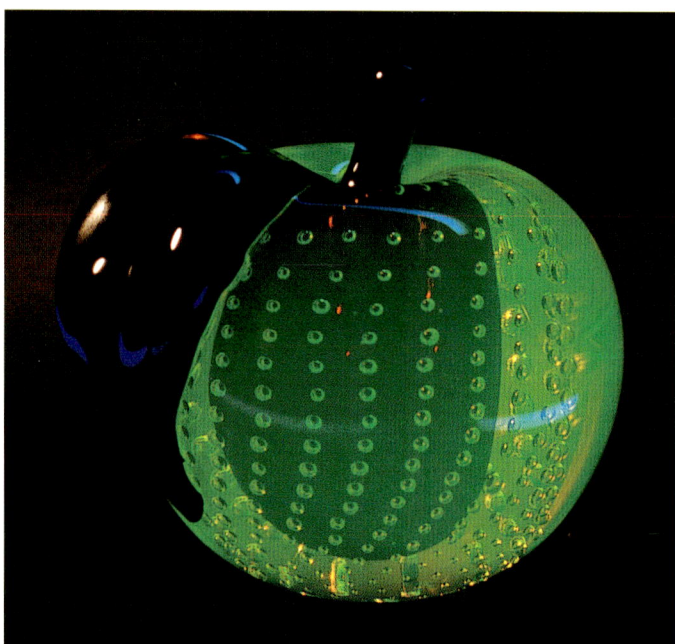

This apple was made by Salviate and Co. on the island of Murano, c. 1950-60s. It is Vaseline bullicante (controlled bubble) with black amethyst sommerso (submerged glass) and leaf and stem. 4.5"h x 4.5"d. $125-150. *Courtesy of Melanie Schonier.*

A ruby sommerso freeform Italian art glass ashtray, c. 1950s. 3"h x 3.5"d. $80-100. *Courtesy of Cindy and Ben Burchfield.*

Vaseline Glass from Europe 147

An amorphous Italian art glass whimsey, Vaseline with blue sommerso, c. 1950s. This unusual piece weighs seven pounds. It has an indention in one side that your hand will fit in. It could be used as a change holder or a giant paperweight. 4.25"h x 7"d. $150-175. *Courtesy of Bill McFarling.*

Overshot vases, European, c. 1880s. The vase on the left is clear shading to cranberry with canary rigaree and feet. 7"h. $175-200. The vase on the right is clear shading to peach with canary rigaree and handles, 6.75"h x 4.1"w. $175-200. *Courtesy of Kelvin Russell and Debra Jennings.*

Pedestal bowl and candlesticks, Italian, c. 1920s. Salviati or Barovier possibly made this pedestal bowl with prunts and matching candlesticks. All stems are clear crystal with gold inclusions. Bowl, 8.25"h x 12"d x 6.37"b. Candlestick, 5.5"h x 3.75"b. $700-800 set. *Courtesy of Melanie Schonier.*

A Victorian 11" centerpiece with original attached stand. European, c. 1880s. The Vaseline overshot bowl shades to cranberry. A gorgeous piece. $800-1000. *Courtesy of Betty and Del Kerr.*

Chapter VI
Uranium Glass

This chapter is for those readers who enjoy the greener colors of glass that fluoresce bright green under ultra-violet light (black light). This glass is often referred to as Green Vaseline. The author prefers the broader term Uranium glass. The term Uranium glass applies to all glass that contains uranium and fluoresces. All pieces in this section are varying shades of green under normal light except for the Burmese epergne. There are other colors like blue, pink, and red that have enough uranium in the formula to make the pieces fluoresce green under black light. Custard and Burmese also contain uranium and will fluoresce green. All of these types of glass can be collectively referred to as Uranium glass.

This large frosted three mold vase has a bird and grain motif, possibly Phoenix or Consolidated, c. 1920s. 10.5"h. $150-175. *Courtesy of Melanie Schonier.*

Coinspot pitcher by Jefferson Glass Co., c. 1905. This pitcher is definitely light green under normal light. 9"h x 6.5"d. $150-180. *Courtesy of Cindy and Ben Burchfield.*

Poppy vase by Tiffin, c. 1920s. This is the Reflex Green vase. It was also made in canary. 9"h. $100-135. *Courtesy of Melanie Schonier.*

Uranium Glass 149

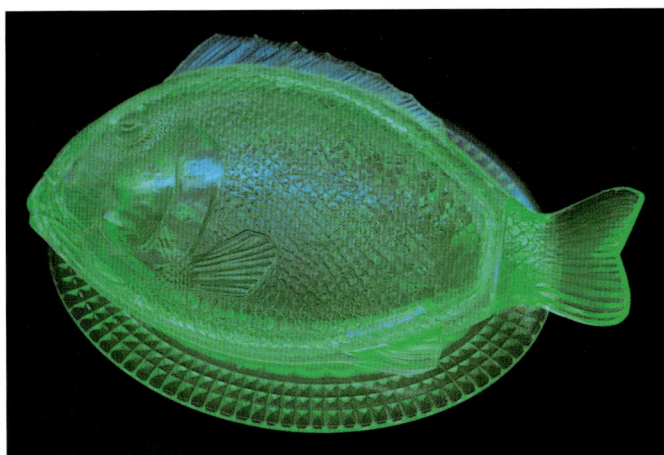

L. G. Wright fish, c. 1937. According to Red Roetteis, Island Mould Co., which became Weisher Mould Co., Wheeling, West Virginia, made this mold for L. G. Wright. It has not been reproduced in this color. 2.75"h x 8"l x 5"w. $125-150. *Courtesy of W. C. "Red" Roetteis.*

A frosted European scent bottle with enamel decoration and ground and polished pontil, c. 1880s. 8"h x 3.4"d. $75-95. *Courtesy of Lena Lou Staton.*

A five piece jade green uranium glass, art deco shaped pitcher with applied cobalt blue handle and matching glasses, c. 1930s. Pitcher, 6.75"h. Tumblers, 4.25"h x 2.5"d. $200-250 set. *Courtesy of Melanie Schonier.*

Rockwell Co. vanity set decorated with oriental motif, c. 1925. The frosted blanks possibly made by Cambridge or Tiffin have silver overlay and bear the etched Rockwell shield. Tray, 11"l x 7"w. Octagon powder box, 2.5"h x 3.5"d. Footed covered dish, 6"h x 5"d. $550-600 set. *Courtesy of Melanie Schonier.*

A cased stick vase with Lily of the Valley enamel decoration and a ground and polished pontil, possibly English, c. 1880s. 4"h x 1.5"sq.b. $50-70. *Courtesy of Melanie Schonier.*

English frosted figural mermaid candlesticks by Bagley, c. 1930s. 8.5"h. $250-275 pr. *Courtesy of Melanie Schonier.*

Figural vanity set. A mermaid/man marine motif vanity tray and matching boxes by Bagley, c. 1930s. Tray, 14"l x 10.5"w. Large box, 5"h x 4.5"d. Small box, 3.75"h x 3.5"d. $450-500 set. *Courtesy of Melanie Schonier.*

Another view of the Bagley vanity set tray.

Uranium Glass 151

Burmese three lily *Diamond Lace* epergne by Fenton, c. 1985. There were only five hundred of these epergnes made. This Burmese epergne is shown in this book to illustrate how glass other than Vaseline will fluoresce bright green under black light if it contains uranium in the glass formula. 10"h x 11"d. $450-500. *Courtesy of Kelvin Russell and Debra Jennings.*

Opalescent *Stripe Optic* biscuit jar. Probably American, c. 1880s-90s. 7"h with lid x 4.5"d. $200-250. *Courtesy of Kelvin Russell and Debra Jennings.*

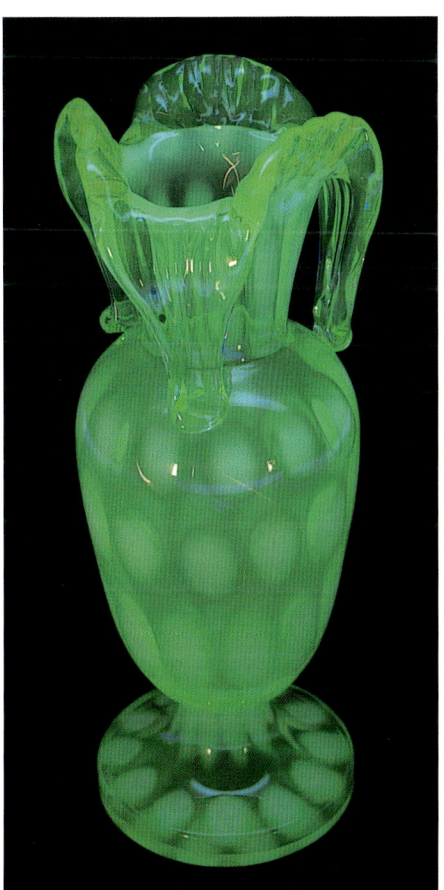

Opalescent *Coin Spot* vase, possibly Czech, c. 1917. 8.75"h x 3.2"b. $110-130. *Courtesy of Kelvin Russell and Debra Jennings.*

Beaded drape biscuit jar. Possibly Pittsburgh Lamp & Glass, c. 1880s. 8"h x 6"d. $350-400. *Courtesy of Kelvin Russell and Debra Jennings.*

Very unusual pair of matching 16" beaded drape Victorian ewers with brass finish collar and feet. Possibly Pittsburgh Lamp & Glass, c. 1880s. The decoration on the metal has an Art Nouveau flare. It is rare to find a set like this. $1400-1800 pr. *Courtesy of Betty and Del Kerr.*

A very unusual Victorian whimsical rubina threaded open front egg with ornate applied leaf and stem that fluoresce. The leaf and stem are green under normal light. Possibly English, c. 1880s-90s. 8.5"h x 4.5"w. $600-800. *Courtesy of Betty and Del Kerr.*

A 12" bride's bowl in a handled stand. The white ruffled bowl is cased with "Green Vaseline" that shades to cranberry on the inside and is decorated with gold and cranberry enameling. Possibly English, c. 1880s-90s. $650-750. *Courtesy of Betty and Del Kerr.*

Uranium Glass 153

Victorian centerpiece, a white bowl cased with peach on the inside. The rolled, pie crust edge is "Green Vaseline." The bowl is highly enameled and is mounted on a whimsical child's stand. Possibly Moser, c. 1880s-90s. $1300-1600. *Courtesy of Betty and Del Kerr.*

Art glass vases, possibly by Boston & Sandwich, c. 1880s-90s. These vases have clear rigaree on the sides and gold and orange decorations. 10.75"h x 4"d. $175 ea. *Courtesy of Kelvin Russell and Debra Jennings.*

Dugan Glass Co. vases. Opalescent vase on left, c. 1908. 14.25"h x 3.65"b. $70-80. Opalescent *Plain Panels* vase on right, c. 1912. 12.5"h x 3.65"b. $60-70. *Courtesy of Kelvin Russell and Debra Jennings.*

154 Uranium Glass

An enameled cordial with hand painted convalaria flower decoration, possibly Bohemian, c. 1890s. 3"h x 1.6"d. $20-25. *Courtesy of Kelvin Russell and Debra Jennings.*

The remaining pieces in this chapter are from the collection of Ulrich Dollinger of Heroldsberg, Germany and are described in his words. Mr. Dollinger, a geologist, has a collection of four thousand pieces of uranium glass and is the author of a book on this subject, titled *Uranglas Uranglasuren*. This photo shows a flint water goblet with hand painted convalaria flower decorations, possibly Bohemian. 5"h x 2.5"d x 2.85"b. $100-150. *Courtesy of Ulrich Dollinger.*

Pressed glass footed water beaker, Bohemian, c. 1902s. 4.5"h x 2"d x 2.45"b. $100. *Courtesy of Ulrich Dollinger.*

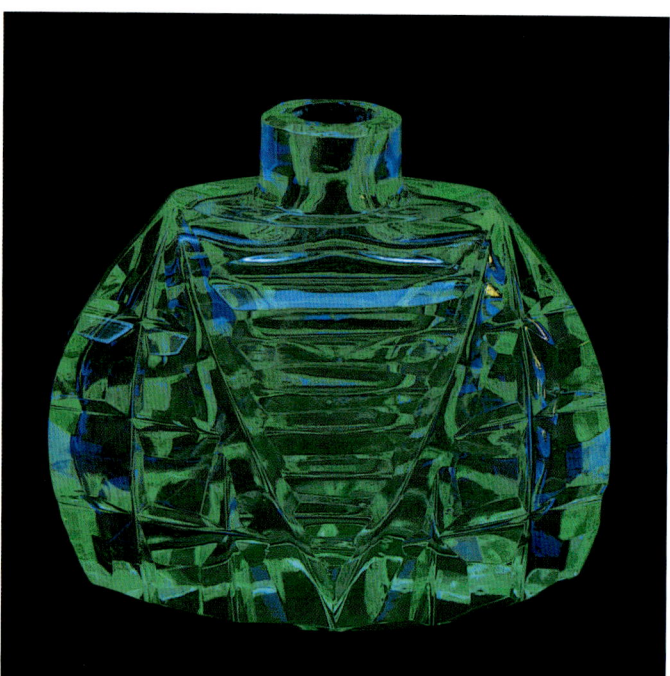

A sniffer bottle for tobacco product (snuff), probably German, c. 1930s. The bottom and edges are ground very smooth. Two views are shown, one under black light and one without black light. 2"h x 2.3"l x 1.1"w. $50-60. *Courtesy of Ulrich Dollinger.*

Uranium Glass 155

Salt, pepper, and mustard set on a black base, possibly Dutch or Belgian. The tops are Bakelite. Very common household and restaurant item in the Netherlands, c. 1920-30s. Base, 4.85"l x 2.75"w. Salt, 2.3"h. Pepper, 3.5"h. Mustard, 1.9"h x 1.42"d. $50-60 set. *Courtesy of Ulrich Dollinger.*

Pressed glass stippled salad bowl, possibly Swedish. The design shows Alpine dancers alternating with a single man dressed in lederhose (shorts made out of leather). 2.6"h x 7"d. $40-60. *Courtesy of Ulrich Dollinger.*

A Bohemian powder jar and perfume, possibly Moser, c. 1920-27. The pieces are cut and ground and have a decorative gold band of mythological figures mainly warriors (Amazon warriors). Perfume with top, 6"h x 3.3"d. Powder jar, 5.25"h x 4.75"d. $200-250 set. *Courtesy of Ulrich Dollinger.*

Wine glasses, possibly German, c. 1810. These glasses have oval shaped bowls with twelve polished panels, cut floral design garlands on the sides and back, and leafed branches around a coat of arms with a helmet and an owl on top. 5.1"h x 2.7"b. $500 ea. *Courtesy of Ulrich Dollinger.*

A Dutch girl satin flower centerpiece. This piece sits in a bowl of water and fresh flowers are put around the frog. Two views are shown for detail. 5.75"h x 4.2"d. $200-250. *Courtesy of Ulrich Dollinger.*

Glossary

Acid-Etching. A method using hydrofluoric acid to decorate glass. The acid eats away exposed surfaces thus forming a design in the glass. It resembles engraving but is flatter.

Air Bubbles. Flaws which occur in a piece of glassware when the glass is being formed by the mixture of various chemicals. Many manufacturers have used the bubbles as a way of creating a new design, and may have deliberately placed bubbles inside a glass design.

Annealing. The process of letting the glass gradually cool so that it is stronger than it might normally be if there were rapid cooling. It is a process performed in a special kiln that allows the glass to slowly reach room temperature.

Applied Glass. A separate gather of glass attached to the main gather during blowing and shaping or immediately after pressing.

Blown Glass. Refers to a type of glass made by the process of blowing air into a pipe attached to molten glass. The glass can be blown by mouth or machine into a mold or formed "freehand."

Bullicante. Air bubbles placed in a regular pattern in the glass.

Cane. Glass rods sliced so that sections of polychrome patterns can be used in mosaic glass or used in striped glass and twisted filigree.

Cased Glass. Glassware that is covered with one or more layers of colored glass. It can be made either by blowing the inner layer into each succeeding outer layer while hot or dipping the gather into molten glass of another color.

Cutting. There are two basics ways in which glass is cut. Smoothing the edge or rim of the glass by melting is the hot method. Smoothing the edge or rim of the glass through a sanding process is the cold method. The cutting method is also used to decorate glass by machine or hand.

Decorating. Cold glass can be decorated by: acid washing, cutting, engraving, etching, frosting, and painting. Some techniques for decorating hot glass are applied relief, crackling, design transfer, lacing, molding, overlaying, pressing, and ribbing.

Engraving. A method using a rapidly rotating stone or copper wheel and an abrasive mixture to decorate glass. The abrasions are shallower than with cutting and have more detail.

Furnace Decorated Glass. Refers to a process of hot glass decoration used by glass blowers. Some forms of furnace decoration include prunts, external ribbing, and threading.

Iridescent Finish. A rainbow-like colored finish sprayed on while the glass is warm. This finish is found on Carnival Glass and art glass.

Lacy-Pattern Glass. Pressed glass characterized by a stippled background and a complex scroll-and-flower design. It was produced from the mid-1820s to mid-1840s.

Millefiori. A thousand flower design created by embedding slices of multicolored canes in clear glass.

Mold. A two, three, or four piece metal or wooden holder used to shape molten glass.

Mold-Marks. When looking at molded glassware, one may be able to see seams in the glass left by the process of shaping the glass and not removed by the manufacturer.

Nappy. A nineteenth century term used by manufacturers to describe small bowls of various shapes.

Opalescent Glass. Glass having a bluish-white, translucent color resembling an opal. When held to a very strong light it will show red highlights.

Ormolu. Ornate metal filigree holders.

Pontil Mark. A rough mark, also called punty, left on the bottom of a piece of blown glass after it has been broken off of the pontil rod.

Pressed Glass. Molten glass pressed into a mold that provides the finished shape and pattern is referred to as pressed glass.

Repoussé. Shaped or ornamented with patterns in relief made by hammering or pressing on the reverse side, especially metal (repoussé decoration).

Rigaree. A piece of glass applied to an object for decoration.

Rubina Verde. A term used to describe the color combination of canary and ruby.

Salver. A term used in the eighteenth and nineteenth centuries to describe a tray or platter on a high stem. This piece could be used for desserts, tea sandwiches, or visiting cards.

Sommerso. Submerged glass in which large colored glass shapes or small particles are encased in clear or different colored thick glass.

Bibliography

Arwas, Victor. *Glass Art Nouveau to Art Deco.* New York: Harry N. Abrams, Inc., 1987.

Bell, John. *Coals to Newcastle.* England.

Boyd's Crystal Art Glass. *Boyd's Crystal Art Glass, The Tradition Continues.* Cambridge, Ohio.

Bredehoft, Neila, and Tom Bredehoft. *Hobbs, Brockunier & Co. Glass.* Paducah, Kentucky: Collector Books, 1997.

Co-Operative Flint Glass Co. Beaver Falls, Pa.

Davis, Sue C. *The Picture Book of Vaseline Glass, Revised & Expanded Second Edition.* Atglen, Pa: Schiffer Publishing, Ltd., 2001.

Dollinger, Ulrich. *Uranglas, Uranglasuren.* © 2000 Bergbau- und Industriemuseum Ostbayern.

Edwards, Bill, & Mike Carwile. *Standard Encyclopedia of Opalescent Glass, 3rd Edition.* Paducah, Kentucky: Collector Books, 1999.

Florence, Gene. *Degenhart Glass & Paperweights.* Cambridge, Ohio: Degenhart Paperweight and Glass Museum, Inc., 1982.

Glickman, Jay L., & Terry Fedosky. *Yellow-Green Vaseline! A Guide to the Magic Glass, Revised Edition.* Marietta, Ohio: Antique Publications, 1998.

Grover, Ray, & Lee Grover. *Art Glass Nouveau.* Rutland, Vermont: Charles E. Tuttle Company, 1970.

Heacock, William. *Encyclopedia of Victorian Colored Pattern Glass Book 1 Toothpick Holders from A to Z.* Marietta, Ohio: Antique Publications, 2nd edition, 1976.

Heacock, William. *Fenton Glass The First Twenty-Five Years.* Marietta, Ohio: O-Val Advertising Corp., 1978.

Heacock, William. *Fenton Glass The Second Twenty-Five Years.* Marietta, Ohio: O-Val Advertising Corp., 1980.

Heacock, William. *Fenton Glass The Third Twenty-Five Years.* Marietta, Ohio: O-Val Advertising Corp., 1989.

Heacock, William. *1000 Toothpick Holders.* Marietta, Ohio: Antique Publications, 1977.

Heacock, William. *Rare & Unlisted Toothpick Holders.* Marietta, Ohio: Antique Publications, 1984.

Heacock, William. *Victorian Colored Pattern Glass Book III.* Marietta, Ohio: Antique Publications, 1976.

Heacock, William. *Victorian Colored Pattern Glass Book 6 Oil Cruets From A to Z.* Marietta, Ohio: Antique Publications, 1981.

Heacock, William, and Fred Bickenhauser. *Victorian Colored Pattern Glass Book 5 U.S. Glass from A to Z.* Marietta, Ohio: Antique Publications, 1978.

Heacock, William, & JoAnn Elmore. *Opalescent Glass from A to Z Books 2 and 9 Revised.* Marietta, Ohio: Antique Publications, 2000.

Heacock, William, and Patricia Johnson. *5,000 Open Salts A Collector's Guide.* Marietta, Ohio: Antique Publications, 1995.

Heacock, William, James Measell, and Berry Wiggins. *Dugan/Diamond The Story of Indiana, Pennsylvania, Glass.* Marietta, Ohio: Antique Publications, 1993.

Heacock, William, James Measell, and Berry Wiggins. *Harry Northwood The Early Years 1881-1900.* Marietta, Ohio: Antique Publications, 1990.

Higby, Lola, and Wayne Higby. *Bryce, Higbee and J. B. Higbee Glass.* Marietta, Ohio: Antique Publications, 1998.

Intercon Arts. *Glass.* Miami, Florida: Intercon Arts, 1984.

Jenks, Bill, and Jerry Luna. *Early American Pattern Glass 1850-1910.* Radnor, Pennsylvania: Wallace-Homestead Book Company, 1990.

Jenks, Bill, Jerry Luna, and Darryl Reilly. *Identifying Pattern Glass Reproductions.* Radnor, Pennsylvania: Wallace-Homestead, 1993.

Krause, Gail. *The Encyclopedia of Duncan Glass.* Tallahassee, Florida: Father & Son Associates, 1997.

Lee, Ruth Webb. *Early American Pressed Glass.* New York: The Ferris Printing Company, 1946.

Lee, Ruth Webb. *Victorian Glass.* Wellesley Hills 81, Massachusetts: Lee Publications, 1944.

McCain, Mollie Helen. *The Collector's Encyclopedia of Pattern Glass.* Paducah, Kentucky: Collector Books, 1982.

McKearin, George S., and Helen McKearin. *American Glass.* Bonanza Books, New York, New York, 1989.

Madeley, John, & John Shetlar. *American Iridescent Stretch Glass.* Paducah, Kentucky: Collector Books, 1999.

Measell, James. *Fenton Glass The 1980s Decade.* Marietta, Ohio: Antique Publications, 1996.

Measell, James, and W.C. "Red" Roetteis. *The L.G. Wright Glass Company.* Marietta, Ohio: Antique Publications, 1997.

Metz, Alice Hulett. *Early American Pattern Glass.* Paducah, Kentucky: Collectors Books, 2000.

Metz, Alice Hulett. *Much More Early American Pattern Glass.* Paducah, Kentucky: Collectors Books, 2000.

Morris, Barbara. *Victorian Table Glass and Ornaments.* London, England: Barrie & Jenkins Ltd., 1978.

National Cambridge Collectors, Inc. *The Cambridge Glass Co.* Paducah, Kentucky: Collector Books, 1991.

Pendergrass, Paula, & Sherry Riggs. *Glass Candleholders.* Atglen, Pa.: Schiffer Publishing, Ltd., 2001.

Phillips, Phoebe. *Encyclopedia of Glass.* Great Britain: Octopus Books Limited, 1981.

Piña, Leslie. *Fifties Glass.* Atglen, Pennsylvania. Schiffer Publishing Ltd., 1997.

Piña, Leslie, and Jerry Gallagher. *Tiffin Glass 1914-1940.* Atglen, Pa.: Schiffer Publishing, Ltd., 1996.

Revi, Albert Christian. *Nineteenth Century Glass.* New York City, New York: Galahad Books, 1967.

Richardson, David E. *Glass Collector's Digest.* Marietta, Ohio: The Glass Press, Inc., 1997.

Shuman III, John A. *The Collector's Encyclopedia of American Art Glass.* Paducah, Kentucky: Collector Books, 1988.

Slack, Raymond. *English Pressed Glass 1830-1900.* London, England: Barrie & Jenkins Ltd., 1987.

Teal, Sr., Ron, *Albany Glass – Model Flint Glass Company of Albany, Indiana.* Marietta, Ohio: Antique Publications, 1997.

Thompson, Jenny. *The Identification of English Pressed Glass 1842-1908.* Kendal, Cumbria: Dixon Printing Co. Ltd., 2000.

Truitt, Robert, and Deborah Truitt. *Collectible Bohemian Glass Vol. II 1915-1945.* Kensington, Md.: B&D Glass, 1998.

Truitt, Robert, and Deborah Truitt. *Collectible Bohemian Glass 1880-1940.* Kensington, Md.: B&D Glass 1995.

Thuro, Catherine M.V. *Oil Lamps II Glass Kerosene Lamps.* Paducah, Kentucky: Collector Books, 1992.

Thuro, Catherine M.V. *Oil Lamps The Kerosene Era in North America.* Radnor, Pennsylvania: Wallace-Homestead, 1992.

Webber, Norman W. *Collecting Glass.* New York City, New York: Arco Publishing Company, 1978.

Whitmyer, Margaret, and Kenn Whitmyer. *Bedroom & Bathroom Glassware.* Paducah, Kentucky: Collector Books, 1990.

Whitmyer, Margaret, and Kenn Whitmyer. *Fenton Art Glass.* Paducah, Kentucky: Collector Books, 1996.